Secrets of a Serial En

Nature of a Social Science

Secrets of a Serial Entrepreneur

A Business Dragon's Guide to Success

SHAF RASUL

CAPSTONE

This edition first published 2010

© 2010 Shaf Rasul

Registered office
Capstone Publishing Ltd. (A Wiley Company), The Atrium, Southern Gate, Chichester, West Sussex, PO19 8SQ, United Kingdom

For details of our global editorial offices, for customer services and for information about how to apply for permission to reuse the copyright material in this book please see our website at www.wiley.com.

Wiley also publishes its books in a variety of electronic formats. Some content that appears in print may not be available in electronic books.

Designations used by companies to distinguish their products are often claimed as trademarks. All brand names and product names used in this book are trade names, service marks, trademarks or registered trademarks of their respective owners. The publisher is not associated with any product or vendor mentioned in this book. This publication is designed to provide accurate and authoritative information in regard to the subject matter covered. It is sold on the understanding that the publisher is not engaged in rendering professional services. If professional advice or other expert assistance is required, the services of a competent professional should be sought.

Library of Congress Cataloguing-in-Publication Data is available.

ISBN 9781907312519

A catalogue record for this book is available from the British Library.

Set in 11/16pt Stone Informal ITC by Sparks (www.sparkspublishing.com)
Printed in Great Britain by TJ International Ltd

CONTENTS

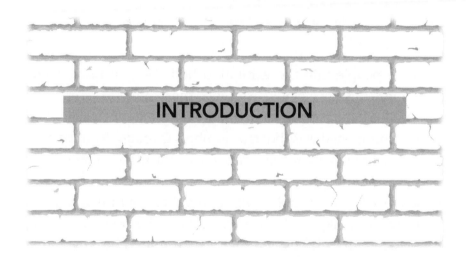

INTRODUCTION

Being an entrepreneur means being in the risk business. You will make some mistakes, and pay for them, but in the end you are your own person and the successes you achieve make up for the difficulties you've met and overcome on the way.

Show me an entrepreneur who tells you they have never got it wrong and I'll show you someone who has started to believe their own propaganda. Making mistakes and learning from them is an unavoidable part of the life of someone who is trying to make a lot of money out of setting up or buying and selling companies.

Here are two quick examples to illustrate my point.

I was once involved in a company that sold exhibition space to suppliers of products in the IT industry. It was doing well but very quickly went downhill when I made a simple mistake. I decided that expansion and growth would be best achieved by increasing the volume of people coming to the exhibitions. I thought that reducing the price of entry might help and took that strategy to its logical conclusion – we stopped asking people to pay anything at all to gain entry. The idea was that it would bring a lot more people into the exhibition hall. This, in turn, would bring more business to our customers, the exhibition stand holders, and we in turn could charge more for the stand space. What actually happened was that the numbers through the front door went up all right – up to ten times (particularly on a Sunday) but the people coming in were less interested in buying IT products. Some of them were simply coming in out of the rain and out of curiosity. That might not sound so bad but the genuine customers were fed up with pushing their way through the crowds and the exhibitors said that the extra people were wasting their time and, of course, stealing stock! It was a classic case of the laws of diminishing returns – and unexpected consequences.

What did I learn from that? That it's not just customer footfall that makes a business successful, it's attracting the people most likely to buy. Salespeople call it 'qualifying the prospects' and it's a topic I will return to later.

It was probably a reasonable risk to take, but it sure didn't come off. But it wasn't a catastrophe; we could recover the goodwill of our customers and get back to business as it was before. So, a mistake and one I could learn from but not terminal.

Contrast this with another entrepreneur who made a mistake. He and his business partners were young men who knew a particular market very well. They were party people and they knew what attracted young people of their age into pubs and clubs. They decided to use that information to set up the sort of pub that they themselves liked to go to – loud music and low lighting.

So, they opened the doors of their new enterprise with a triumphant flourish and the party animals of the town came flooding in. Within a few weeks they had a packed venue and the cash was rolling into the tills. Everything was top quality with no expense spared. There were a lot of customers, so they needed a lot of expensive doormen. This kind of crowd didn't want to wait long for a drink, so they had lots of bar staff. They had the top DJs, and regular parties both for the customers and also for the staff after work.

Unfortunately, the concepts of profit, loss and cash flow were passing them by. They did not understand profit margins – their strategy was to pitch prices at what people would pay, regardless of the cost of the drink. They took the money out of the till, and bought fast cars and houses they couldn't really afford as well as the electronic toys of the day.

And, of course, it fell apart. In short, they spent the money in the till without realizing how much of it really belonged to them after costs and overheads. Because it was their business they confused the profits of the business with their own personal profits. The end of this story is bitter sweet. The bad news was that they shut up shop, gave the keys of the pub back to their lender and left a bunch of suppliers with unpaid bills. The good news was that they learnt from the experience, were not deterred by what had happened and started again. This time they knew the basics of business, they still understood the market they were aiming at and they went on to make a small fortune out of pubs and clubs. They are now seasoned entrepreneurs – all the more so because they know what it is to pick yourself up, dust yourself off and plunge straight back into the saloon fight.

In the first chapter of this book I will help you decide if you have what it takes to be an entrepreneur.

There's a part of me that thinks anyone can be a successful risk-taking entrepreneur. It's interesting that Duncan Bannatyne, one of the Dragons in the Den, wrote a book called *Anyone Can Do It*, and the founders of Coffee Republic, a successful chain of coffee bars and concessions (and nothing to do with *Dragons' Den*), wrote their story and guess what they called it: *Anyone Can Do It*!

I had a conversation with a friend on the topic. He claimed that he could never be a millionaire because he wasn't very good with money. Now, I personally believe that you don't have to be a financial genius to make a million but on the other hand you do have to get the financial basics right, otherwise you run the risk of imitating the folk who started their own bar. I'll be taking a look at what entrepreneurs are really made of in Chapter 1 and at the financial basics needed in Chapter 6.

Getting a head start

People who feel motivated or even compelled to set up their own business are quite likely to have been brought up in a family firm or in a family where at least one of the breadwinners ran their own business.

I was brought up in a family that owned and ran a newsagent's 'corner' shop. I did my first paper round when I was ten and heard my parents talk about the good times and, more worryingly, the tough times that affect all business owners at some point or another. I learnt a lot from that experience; I may not have realized it at the time but profit, how much we could safely draw from the business, and cash flow, money received minus money spent over a given period of time, were concepts with which I was very familiar before I set up my first enterprise.

I learnt a lot from the family business:

- the basics of how money works
- knowing that working smart is as important as working hard
- that you shouldn't over extend on borrowings
- to keep a tight control of the finances
- to keep your finger on the pulse all the time; if you look away something will go wrong
- the importance of knowing your customers.

Finally, the most important lesson I learned was that I knew I wanted to do something on a much bigger scale than the traditional family firm. I dared to go big.

So does that mean you have to have grown up with a family business in order to understand entrepreneurism? No of course not. I'm just saying it helps. It doesn't matter if you grew up in a home where your parents worked in corporate companies or institutions – it doesn't affect your ability to think like an entrepreneur. After all, many managers in large corporations demonstrate entrepreneurism and innovativeness on a daily basis. The first part of learning the basics of being an entrepreneur is being prepared to listen to other people. Perhaps most importantly, you should talk to people running small businesses so as to get a handle on the mindset of the person running their own thing. There's no information or advice as fresh and useful as the opinions of someone whose livelihood depends on their daily business. It's not hard to come by that kind of wisdom either; people who run their own businesses love talking about them. They will all give you some information that's the same as everyone else, and some that is peculiar to what they are doing. So, the next time you go into a restaurant, and it's quiet, ask the owner how their business is doing, what is going well and what, if anything, is worrying them. Do the same in your local IT shop; talk to social acquaintances and so on. You will be surprised how much real, practical information you can pick up.

Anyone can do it

As an entrepreneur, I believe I have the ability to think outside the box; spotting, for example, opportunities that others don't. Perhaps, too, I take risks that no one else would even consider and I instinctively 'get' the benefit behind that basic business principle – the higher the risk, the higher the return. I also relish the sense of accomplishment and enjoy the financial rewards that come with success. Some people say that I was born to be a millionaire and in some ways this may be true. However, I believe that I was born to be an entrepreneur and along the way I made a few million.

How do I have the nerve to write this book? Well, to be fair to me, I only worked for a company for an hour and three-quarters. I knew after that time that it just wasn't for me to sit at a desk and make money for other people.

Since then I have bought, started and sold businesses. I have made loads of mistakes along the way and I'll tell you about them as well, so that you can learn the same lessons as I did. But I've also had some successes too: after all, I was a multi-millionaire before I was thirty. That's partly why I have the nerve to write this book; I've got lots of experience. And then there's the huge fun and privilege of being a Dragon in the Den. Through this I have looked at the many ideas of would-be entrepreneurs, some great, some not so great, looking for financial investment and a sounding board for their ideas from people who have been involved in small business start-ups. Passing on what I've learnt in the Den should also be helpful.

Helpful to you, I hope. You've bought or borrowed this book so I am making the assumption that either you want to start the process of becoming a successful entrepreneur or you're already in business and want to add to the profitability of your current company. I hope after you have read the book that you will also want to sell your businesses, buy some others and make a lot of money. You can certainly learn some entrepreneurial skills; so I believe millionaires can be made as well as born. In my opinion a little bit of talent can go a very long way!

So, the key topics of this book are:

- buy the right businesses
- start your own business
- make a business profitable fast
- sell businesses for a profit.

Buy the right businesses: this involves analysing the position of a company quickly. It's a mixture of gut feeling and good mathematics. Remember, buying companies is a competitive business – if it looks good to me, it'll look good to other entrepreneurs or another Dragon, so you have to act fast. The analysis is not just the numbers, although I like to get to them as fast as possible, it's also about the person with the idea; do they have what I call business nous and can I trust them?

Start your own business: when people come to the *Dragons' Den* they're not just after the money. They want a mentor. A lot of what I bring to a business now is not investment but my value as a sounding board for getting ideas off the ground. Like many entrepreneurs I also help people get their businesses going even when I'm not an investor. I'm interested in helping potential entrepreneurs and do a lot of charity work in this area, mentoring and encouraging young people.

Make a business profitable fast: look, we're in a hurry, remember ... We have invested money in a business and we want it back with a healthy profit as soon as possible. If it was unprofitable when you bought it, as many of my best success stories have been, then you need to know the tricks of the trade for turning it round into a profitable concern quickly. If it's making money at the moment but not enough to attract a buyer then you need to work out how to increase your profitability – it can be done but the longer you leave it the less real return you're making.

Sell businesses for a profit: it is not necessary to sell the whole business at first; it might have some assets in it that you want to maintain an interest in, or the buyer may want you to stay with the company for a while as part of the terms and conditions of the sale. Indeed, most entrepreneurs are good at sorting out shareholdings without damaging their position. Suppose, for example, you have someone in a company that you wholly own and they are running the part of the business located in the north-west region. Suppose next that they feel that their success in the north-west entitles them to expect some shares in the business they are helping to build. This may well be a sensible reward, but you don't have to give them shares in the holding company. It might make more sense to create Newco Northwest and give them shares in that. (Investors tend to call companies that do not yet exist 'Newcos' until they have a name.) That could improve the profitability of the whole organization and lock the manager into the long-term strategy of the business. In this book we'll look at how you find buyers and negotiate the best deal.

As much as anything else it's about attitude and a willingness to have a go. It's about overcoming that classic fear of failing – it's somehow seen as being better to have never tried to make it than to have a go and fail. I'll give you an example. I once suggested a wager with a friend: I was willing to bet that I could mentor him into achieving success. I was confident that I could make him a millionaire within 2 years. My friend politely declined the offer and dinner conversation progressed to a different topic. Interestingly, I was happy to take the chance that he would make it but he was not happy to take the chance that he might not. I firmly believe that you don't have to be a financial genius to make a million.

I have written the chapter about buying businesses before the one about starting your own business. I have done this for two main reasons. First of all, the intention of an entrepreneur is to build businesses and then sell on all or parts of them to release money to build other businesses or, of course, to retire to sunnier climes. It makes sense, therefore, to think first about what someone buying a business is looking for

I firmly believe that you don't have to be a financial genius to make a million.

– how they will value the assets of a company to weigh up how they could make more money out of them. The second reason is that I want to emphasize that the real fun and profit in being an entrepreneur is to be continuously looking for new opportunities to buy into, put into order and then sell. So I will talk about running and growing businesses and show you the skills you need to do that, but always against the background of buying, selling and moving on.

Features of the book

There are three basic devices I'll be using throughout the book:

Tip from Shaf – Tricks of the Trade

These are tried-and-tested tools and techniques covering a wide range of topics that I have found really work.

FAQ – Frequently Asked Questions

These are questions that I am often asked by my employees, by my business partners and by the people that I mentor and help with their businesses. There are questions too from people who just come up to me in the street with a query about their company, or something that has cropped up in the *Dragons' Den*.

I tried it and …

"These are comments from people who have taken my advice or tried out a trick of the trade. They often give me feedback on how things went, so I think it's useful to pass their experience on too. I have not attributed them to a particular person because they are often an amalgam of things that people have said to me over the years."

Tip from Shaf – Think Outside the Box

Take a simple business decision that you have to make. Perhaps you could try writing your company's vision or your team's slogan as a simple example. Think of what comes immediately to you and then reject that thought; everyone will think of that. Now find an alternative. It will be better and only a few people will think of it. Now reject that and rack your brains to think of a third approach. Now you're thinking outside the box and coming up with an idea or a decision that is unique to you. You can do this for all forward planning or strategic decisions.

Now, let's find out if you are an entrepreneur ...

1

ARE YOU AN ENTREPRENEUR?

Well, are you? There's a harsh school of thought that says 'If you're not in business for yourself already then you're not an entrepreneur.' While it's true that most of the entrepreneurs I know are pretty driven people, many of them did go through an apprenticeship with a big company, learning about business, finance and management, before taking off on their own. So, let's say it's never too late.

It is worth a bit of time to think about what an entrepreneur is and does and to take a close look at yourself before you take the plunge. By the time you've read this chapter you should have a pretty good idea if you are indeed already an entrepreneur or, perhaps more importantly, if you can become one.

Millions of people want to make a million but that doesn't make them entrepreneurs. Thousands of people have an idea for a business, but that doesn't make them entrepreneurs. Hundreds have entirely original ideas with great potential, but that doesn't make them entrepreneurs either. So before you answer the question at the top of this chapter, let's talk a little about just what is – and what isn't – an entrepreneur.

I remember in *Dragons' Den* when we had a chap called Alex with a product he'd invented called the Ladder Buddy and I asked him if he would say he was an entrepreneur. His reply was that 'if creating things and changing things and enjoying changing things is being an entrepreneur, then that's me.' I stopped him and said, 'No, that's an inventor, you're not an entrepreneur.'

Alex had come up with a good idea, he'd done a bit of market research (a subject I'll come back to with a vengeance) and he'd found a gap in the market – but he was not an entrepreneur. He wanted to own the product – it was his 'baby' – and he wanted to make it himself, despite not being from a manufacturing background. I told him that if I were he I would just have licensed the product for someone else to make and sell, but he didn't want to do that. Despite saying this, I still liked his idea and offered him the money he was looking for … but only in return for 70% of the equity of his company. I also told him that the product would be marketed on my terms and my terms only. To his credit, Alex swallowed hard but he accepted the deal – as he admitted himself afterwards he had had a go and taken the idea as far as he could. He was stuck and unable to go further. To get to the next level he needed someone like me. I'm not in the business of making DIY products. I'm in the business of making money. Alex recognized that. Most people don't. Most people can't distinguish entrepreneurial nous from standard good business sense, or having great ideas. This is not to say there's anything wrong with inventiveness or good business sense, just that they are not to be confused with the attitude and aptitudes required to be an entrepreneur. Don't think that just because you've got an idea you're an entrepreneur, because if you confuse your creativity with the ability to make money out of it then you're likely to waste your chances or end up making someone else rich. Assess your strengths, assess your weaknesses, realize where you need help and you're already halfway there.

FAQ – Can't an Accountant Do It?

Q: *Surely I can buy in the knowledge that I lack to run a business? After all, everyone uses accountants to run the financial side of the business.*

A: Only up to a point. Accountants are very good at telling you how you have done in the past. But you can't wait for their 6-monthly reports, which are a month old before you get them, to run your business successfully. That's like driving a car by looking in the rear-view mirror.

A breed apart

There's no doubt about it, entrepreneurs stand out from other people.

I used to be a student at Strathclyde University and, like so many before me, I looked around for a job as soon as I graduated and found one in a legal firm. I worked there for literally two hours before I decided that it wasn't for me. No, I tell a lie, it was probably more like one hour forty-five minutes. I found it difficult to accept – I had people bossing me about and I thought to myself, 'No, it's not going to be like that – I'm going to be my own man owning any business I work in'.

Nothing too unusual about that: there are other people who don't enjoy their jobs much. Lots of people also love their jobs and the security of working for an established company. Not so many of those who dislike what they are doing decide to do something about it and walk out the door.

Within two days I had my own company. It was nothing to do with law either. I had a conversation with a man on a train who talked about his work in an IT department and I thought, that's an interesting business sector, one which is obviously growing and where demand is outstripping supply. So I started an IT business.

Tip from Shaf – Time the Plunge

I'm pretty convinced that the best time to go it alone is when you are young. At this stage the only person you can really damage is yourself. It's much more difficult to take the risk of setting up your own business when you have a spouse and a couple of kids than when you're fresh out of school or college. You may find there is a period in your life, say the time when you have young children, that you have to live through before the window of opportunity opens again.

Looking back on how I started, there are a few lessons to be learnt. Hating my job didn't make me an entrepreneur. If that was all it took then many more of us would be entrepreneurial millionaires! Walking out of my job didn't make me an entrepreneur either, but having the will to walk was part of the process. Finally, starting up my own company was the clear turning point. To get there you don't have to be me, you don't have to look like me and you don't have to sound like me. You might not even have to walk out of that job (not just yet anyway) but you'd better have the ability to make it happen, to actually DO something. So when you ask yourself if you're an entrepreneur, don't ask if you have the hunger to succeed, or a good idea, or even better than average business sense.

All of those are needed, but you'll also need a healthy helping of the following.

Do you have the strength of character to stand out?
Lady luck smiles on ordinary people all the time, right? Wrong. We all wish it were true, and we want it to happen so much that we throw our money away on the lottery hoping it will be us. The only real winner in a lottery is the organizer and beneficiary charities. Entrepreneurs don't trust to luck – they make it happen. To make it big you have to be ready to take the lead and push things through regardless of whether that suits other people or not.

Entrepreneurs don't trust to luck – they make it happen.

There's a popular stereotype of the entrepreneur as a hard-nosed, ruthless, grumpy sort of person. That's not entirely true! You don't have to be rude to be an entrepreneur, but if your first concern is what others will think or whether people will like you or not, then you're going to struggle to drive your own agenda. Just look at the name *Dragons' Den*. I have a reputation for being hard on people on the show, but I'm not out to be rude to anyone. I just weigh the pros and cons of their business proposition and make my judgement. The 'rudeness' that some perceive is because I don't worry about what people want to hear when I give them my verdict, I tell them how I really see it. If you can't do that, or learn to do it, then you'll never really be running your own show, on your own terms and to your own advantage.

Tip from Shaf – Don't Hobble Talent

You will need strength of character to really lead your business and your team. Remember, however, when you and your team are in planning mode, or when you are having meetings about the way ahead or having 'away-days' to really look at forward planning, that you make sure you encourage everyone to contribute their ideas. Always give your team the courtesy of thinking about their ideas and discussing them fully. An entrepreneur doesn't have to be a perfect diplomat, or even much of a democrat, but you should always listen to what the people around you have to say. Surrounding yourself with the right partners is one of the skills you're going to cultivate and having selected good partners you'd be a fool not to listen to them. If the team starts to think that it doesn't matter what they suggest, that you already decided the plan before the session starts, then you will hobble their thinking, make them keep potentially good ideas to themselves and so feel frustrated.

Yes, in the end it's your call; but if you don't consult and never go with someone else's idea then you will end up with a team of 'yes men' whose talent you will never truly tap.

Do you have the self-belief?

Not a shadow of doubt about this one. You have to believe in yourself all the way or nobody else will believe in you either. This goes naturally hand-in-hand with showing strength of character but it's worth pointing out separately because some people believe that by acting like Sir Alan Sugar with a hangover they will automatically become more entrepreneurial. It's not about having 'attitude', it's about having a rock-solid faith in your own abilities, your game plan and your figures. Yes, your game plan and your figures.

There are a lot of successful entrepreneurs with strong characters and it's tempting to get the impression that they got there by force of character alone. But if self-belief is the hallmark of successful people there's a difference between blind self-belief, and unshakeable self-belief based on the confidence that you've done your homework, run your figures, re-run them, and come to the conclusion that you are on to a winner. It's the difference between someone who thinks they're Napoleon because they've just put on the funny hat, and someone who thinks they're Napoleon because outside the door there's a 65,000 man Grande Armée ready to do their bidding. Be sure of yourself by all means, but be sure because you've got the insight, the strategy and the resources, not just because the face in the mirror tells you you're wonderful.

Tip from Shaf – Believe in Yourself, But Get Help from Others

When you are running your own organization you need to stay focused on the big picture of where the business is going, but you also have to keep an eye on the detail. Make sure you have enough knowledge and the courage of your convictions to use, and where necessary, challenge professional and technical advisers. Yes, it means that you have to get down to the nitty gritty from time to time. Anything you learn from accountants or bankers about finance, for example, may be crucial to some later decisions that you make. My message is – don't accept at face value professional advice that gives you a sneaking concern that it is inconsistent with how you want to work. Go over it carefully, get the advisers to explain anything you do not understand and then make your own decision.

Do you believe in your product?
Just believing in yourself is all very well but it really is just the starting point. The next step is to come up with a business idea that you genuinely believe is excellent. If you have doubts about it then others will have doubts too and that may be enough to stall the whole thing. Many of the best entrepreneurial ideas come from people who recognize that they are their own target market. Knowing just why a consumer or client wants the service is a brilliant starting point and will give you the assurance needed to convince others.

Even that is only the first step, however. Truly understanding the worth of your product is a great base to work from but you also need to ensure that other people share your needs or tastes. If you've got the belief in the product, the conviction that there is a market out there, then the rest is a matter of juggling the figures and working out your route to market.

Now let's go back to Alex and his Ladder Buddy again. He understood the product because he realized that it was something he himself would use. He had also looked around the UK and seen that he is not the only bloke with a DIY habit. He'd even looked further afield and seen that if it could work in the UK then it could perhaps make that leap across the Atlantic and in the process make him a very rich man indeed. Yet at that point he got stuck. Why? Because his instinct was to keep the whole project for himself. His self-belief had got him just so far yet he couldn't quite take it to the next level. He had run into the wall of his own limitations and he and his Ladder Buddy couldn't get over it without help. Which brings us to the next crucial belief ...

Do you believe in others?
Alex didn't think of licensing his product because like so many people with a 'brainchild' that is very dear to them, they can't bear to hand it over to the care of someone else.

However, to be really successful you can't just do it on your own. True, there are plenty of successful characters who like to give the impression that they made it to the top without the benefit of any help, but there are very few businesses which manage to be one man industries and hugely successful as well. Even world-beating novelists usually acknowledge the debt they owe to a team of editors and publishers. If you're hoping to make an impact in any area of manufacturing or service provision then you're going to need other people, and for that you need to be a good judge of character.

Life in general, and business in particular, is all about people and once you've made your call then you have to believe in your people as much as you believe in yourself. A lot of entrepreneurs fail not because they have a bad idea, but because they're not ready to trust others. You can only get so far without outside help. If you're so attached to an idea that you can't bear to hand it over to someone else to help you expand it then you're not an entrepreneur, you're an inventor, or a foster parent for a business.

Another group of would be entrepreneurs fail because they don't understand that leaders don't need to be liked. They need to be respected. They may be liked as well, but the first step is to be respected and trusted – which doesn't necessarily mean being popular. The key to being respected (and it often leads to being liked) is to be straight with others, and for me the key that underpins being straight with others is the idea that I'll trust them in return. If I tell someone I believe that they can do something then I mean it (or else they wouldn't be there). People respond well to that kind of trust, they 'step up to the plate' and they become the kind of co-workers you always wanted them to be. Fail to believe in them and they start to believe that they will fail you.

FAQ – Making Mistakes

Q: *I trust my staff. In a recent incident I didn't step in to correct them even though I felt their choice of action was a mistake. I was right, but if I'd stepped in I would have badly undermined them in front of others. So should I let someone make a mistake even though I could have stepped in and stopped the mistake happening?*

A: Yes, in some cases you should let people make mistakes. I don't mean that I would let someone wreck the business, but suppose you and an experienced manager don't agree on how to solve a problem. If the person is sure that they will succeed and wants passionately to do it their way, let them have a go – even if your gut instinct tells you they are wrong. They will learn from their mistakes and become better and more effective managers as a result.

Can you handle it?

Being an entrepreneur is a risky business. It's all about seizing your chances and believing in yourself whatever the odds. People ask me all the time if I've ever had failures and I tell them of course I have. If you're an investor and you make ten investments then, on average, six of them are going to fail, three will break even but it will all be worth it for that one that makes it – and makes it spectacularly. If you're afraid of failing you are much more likely to fail because you won't press home your opportunities. Most people fail for the simple reason that they don't dare have a go in the first place.

Dominic Byrne, Radio 1 presenter and the presenter of *Dragons' Den Online,* once observed to me that the stress looks immense for the people who come on and present to us. Of course it is. Public speaking is a terrifying experience for most of us and the show ramps that up enormously with TV cameras and a scowling bald Scotsman to impress (I'm not talking about co-Dragon Julie here). But what's easy to miss in the shows is that the candidates aren't the only ones under stress. Believe it or not, the Dragons' pulses are racing too. The adrenaline is pumping when we're in that situation. Get it wrong and you lose £50,000 of your own money. If we back a business that folds or miss out on a good opportunity we will be a laughing stock so we have to be careful when we're out there making that decision.

I think failing to attempt something is more of a failure than having a go and not succeeding. But for a lot of us the prospect of failure is more embarrassing and frightening than the idea of doing nothing at all. Instead we prefer to play safe.

There's a problem with 'safe' though. If 'safe' means not taking chances or trying to better our lot then it goes beyond safe and becomes a form of imprisonment. 'Safe' is what keeps us stuck at that desk in a job we hate. You might reasonably think that this book is about getting rich. It's about something a lot more important than that. It's about daring to take your chances and realize your ambitions. To peek out from the cover of 'safe' and decide that you like what you see and that you want to live a more challenging but ultimately more fulfilling life. Of course if you happen to become rich along the way I don't suppose you will be complaining too loudly.

Are you prepared to make the sacrifices it takes?

Thomas Edison famously defined genius as 'one percent inspiration and ninety-nine percent perspiration'. This is as true as it ever was but that sweat takes on many different forms. Being ready to be an entrepreneur means being ready to pay the price, whatever that means: the long hours, the loneliness of going solo or being in command, the investment of all of your savings. Remember that you don't really make your money on an investment until you pull out of it so if you have a long-term exit strategy then make sure you can survive for the time it takes to see it through to fruition.

I don't want to go on too much about the sacrifice: I certainly don't want to put you off; but some people find it difficult to appreciate just what it means to go it on your own. It's not just the risk that you're taking but the small things as well. You're not expecting just how many things will come along that you will have to sort out before you can get back to the main part of your work. A friend of mine gave me a good example of these little things.

'The day after I left my job as a second line manager in a multinational, I was sitting at my desk in my one-roomed office making phone calls to prospective customers. The light above my desk went out; the bulb had gone. Now in my old job I would have told someone in my team about it and somehow, I didn't know how, it would have got replaced. Now, though I was on my own.

'To reach the bulb I needed a ladder; I had no ladder and certainly did not want to spend any money on something like that.

So I went out and borrowed a ladder from a shop nearby. I climbed the ladder and got the bust bulb out. Off I went in my car to a shop that sold bulbs and bought one. Back to the office, replace the bulb and take the ladder back – amount of time wasted – one hour and a quarter.'

So it's hard work and you have to keep yourself and your family going through some difficult times; but everyone I know who has done it has found it worthwhile in the end.

Can you see the devil in the detail? Or does it make your eyes glaze over?

I've said before that just having a good idea doesn't make you an entrepreneur; at least not by itself. In order to get to the next stage you have to take a cold, hard look at the numbers and that's where I think a lot of people let themselves down when they come into the Den. I've said many times that *Dragons' Den* isn't some kind of game show. We're there as genuine investors and I don't care how entertaining an idea is or how charming the person is that's presenting it, if there isn't a gap in the market or if the figures don't add up then I'm not going to put my money behind it.

I always tell the entrepreneurs to know their numbers well before they come on the show. The idea is that they're not selling me a gadget, they're selling me the business idea behind the gadget and that means they must have costings for manufacture and distribution, projected sales and profit margins. These figures are every bit as important as the gadget they are usually cradling lovingly in their arms. The same advice about making sure you have your numbers ready stands for anyone thinking of going into business for themselves. If you can't show me the calculations for long-term predictions, a suitable exit point, a healthy margin and an idea of your total investment and return then you can't call yourself an entrepreneur. If you're unsure about finance then don't worry, help is at hand in Chapter 6.

It's not rocket science, but failing to get to grips with the figures is one of the most fundamental ways of failing to understand your own business. As a result it is also one of the main reasons why people with good business ideas end up filing for bankruptcy.

There are lots of reasons why people don't do the numbers properly. Some people are afraid of the figures themselves. Chapter 6 will give you an idea of what you need to be able to master. If, after reading it, you're still sure that you don't have the necessary skill or temperament to master the finances then you're going to need to find a partner whom you can trust absolutely to help you with the financial side of things.

Too many would-be entrepreneurs fail to fully address the issues of finances and plunge ahead with a vague feeling that somehow the finances will take care of themselves. That could be because of blind self-belief or an overpowering enthusiasm for the business idea. Either way it's a trap. There is a list as long as my arm of smart people with great ideas who don't find business success because they didn't take into account the likely expenses or the plan for the necessary cash flow. Don't be one of those people. If you don't have what it takes to minutely plan your money then get help from someone who does. You wouldn't let your family go short of food for poor financial planning so why would you want to let your business down that way?

How well do you know your markets?

We see this a lot on *Dragons' Den*: our would-be entrepreneurs have ideas and spend a lot of time thinking about them. Then they go out and ask their friends or family what they think. Family and friends don't want to hurt their feelings so they say that it's great. Now our wannabe entrepreneur is firmly convinced that they're on to a winner and the idea becomes an obsession. Even when their family and friends finally beg them to stop (usually because our entrepreneur is about to re-mortgage the house), they've convinced themselves by this time that they are right; there is a huge untapped market out there for their idea. What they haven't done, for a minute, is think about or carry out any market research. The result is that a lot of the ideas we see are frankly ludicrous. They would never work, there's no way anyone would buy them and no investor is ever going to back them. Whatever the wannabe entrepreneur has spent so far has been wasted money but they feel they can't back down now. The next chapter goes into more detail about knowing when to pull out.

There's a fine line here. I said earlier that you have to believe in yourself and not be too willing to please others. But that doesn't mean that you shouldn't find out what others think, just that you have to make the call about what to do with that information. I would say to a lot of the would-be entrepreneurs on the show that instead of talking to family and friends they should first explain their idea to a hundred people they don't know and listen to what they have to say about it. In the days of internet blogs and Twitter, this shouldn't be as hard to do as it may sound. Of course it could be that you have an idea that's ahead of its time and people will struggle to understand its implications. In which case you'll need the strength of character to push forward and make it happen but you will at least now know what kind of obstacles you are up against.

Coming back to the importance of knowing your market: a woman I was mentoring decided to take the market research thing very seriously. She wanted to open a shop on a busy street in a city. She wanted to check the footfall of passers-by going past the premises she was thinking of renting. She sat in her car for most of a day and then noticed something really interesting – it was much busier on the opposite side of the street than on the side her shop was located. She then realized that the busy side was also the sunny side of the street. Acting on that research she rented a shop on the sunny side. Now that's what I call dedication and thank goodness she went to that trouble; customer footfall is of paramount importance in the retail business.

So, market research sounds like it's about consultants and flow charts. However, just pounding the beat like the punter is often the simplest way of seeing things from their point of view and understanding their spending habits.

Are you eternally watchful?

Dominic Byrne, radio DJ and presenter of *Dragons' Den Online*, once asked me what I did to 'switch off' – whether I kicked a ball around in the park or went to the pub like everyone else. I do the kinds of things that other people do, but I told him I didn't understand what he meant by 'switch off'. Because I don't, and I can't. I analyse things all the time.

When we checked into the hotel we were staying at for the programme shoot, the service was a bit slow. As Dominic said himself, all he wanted to do was get to his room, but I wanted to know why nobody was offering to valet park my car. There were three staff members in sight who weren't helping us. Dominic still laughs and accuses me of being permanently engaged in time and motion studies, but I don't see it that way because it's a purely unconscious reaction. He saw some slightly unhelpful staff. I saw several key (and expensive) business resources that happened to be in human form. Those resources were not being used, which meant a huge waste of manpower when they could have been engaged in offering services for the business's customers. If that had been my hotel there would have been a few choice words.

True entrepreneurs don't switch off because they're always looking at businesses they come across (from shops to hotels, from car dealerships to cafes) and asking if they could make them better. It doesn't matter what kind of business it is and what kind of business you are in, they just can't help but analyse other businesses and look for ways they would make them more efficient, more profitable, bigger or leaner. If you don't have this kind of constant curiosity about how other businesses make money then you're probably not going to be able to maximize the return from your own. If you're not interested in other businesses then you should ask yourself if you are really interested in business at all, or whether it is just your own idea that you like. In which case you are, like Alex and his Ladder Buddy, more of an inventor than an entrepreneur and you should seek out someone who is more entrepreneur than inventor in order to make the next step.

Can you balance long-term thinking and planning with short-term action?

In the next section, you will have the opportunity of assessing your own suitability for going into business on your own. I have first to report from my own observations, and from conversations with people who have started businesses successfully, that the top person in a new and growing company needs to have 'two heads'. That can either mean a second head in the form of a partner or, at the risk of developing a borderline split personality, it can mean constantly looking at the business from a different point of view.

The problem is the common one of balancing the pressures of doing business today against the longer-term thinking required to build the dream.

Without a long-term strategy, companies run the risk that the decisions they are making today will have a negative impact on results in the future.

But we have to stay real; business people are always under pressure to carry out urgent day-to-day tasks. They have to meet today's objectives and overcome short-term problems. They have to respond to their customers, deal with staff issues, address an online problem and so on. Everyone is at some time involved in this day-to-day operational work or short-term planning. In a fast-moving environment it is little wonder that planning for the future tends to take second place.

If these statements are true for all organizations, they are all the more so for start-ups and small companies. A terrific-sounding long-term strategy is nothing short of disastrous if it runs the risk of running out of cash in the short term. Cash flow is lifeblood for a company and for a small business with smaller cash flow it is much easier to run dry than for a large organization with cash and credit lines sloshing around all over the shop. On the other hand, diverting cash away from strategic projects just to fund the day-to-day may cripple any hope for expansion. The two needs must be weighed up to decide where the biggest threat lies, but bear in mind that you only have the luxury of worrying about long-term problems if you survive the short-term ones.

So, we come back to the need for two heads. The top of any start-up company needs someone with a 'can do' and 'do it now' attitude – it needs someone who will discuss a problem, find a solution and immediately pick up the telephone to start imple-menting it. As for the solutions themselves, expect to need some fancy footwork at times, just to keep the business afloat. No one has solved the particular problems you are about to face; there is no precedent as to the outcome of your particular situation, so one of your two heads has to spot solutions or activities that would be described by some managers in large companies as completely 'off the wall'.

And yet, no one built a business without thinking about the fu-ture and how the future impacts on what we do now – the second head.

Some people, many of them entrepreneurs, can simulate the two mindsets inside their one brain, reacting, ducking and weaving with the best of them but also from time to time checking that they are not mortgaging the future or taking short-term meas-ures that endanger the long-term goal. Others find themselves a partner and form teams of two where one person is clearly the 'let's do it' go-getter, and the other is the more reticent, 'just a minute, let's think this through' person. So, think on. Can you accommodate both mindsets simultaneously, or do you need a partner or a right-hand man or woman to balance your business?

The 'Are you an entrepreneur?' quiz

Here is a series of questions to ask yourself and some observa-tions about your answers. Try to do the quiz as honestly as you can and mark the answers that you have given. Then check them out with someone at work or at home who knows you well to see if they confirm your view of yourself. Getting this kind of feed-back from a third party is invaluable. Chose someone you trust, ideally two or three people, and ask them to be as honest as possible.

1 Are you a self starter?
   a Absolutely.
   b I prefer a bit of guidance at first to be sure I'm doing the right thing.
   c No; when I think about it I like someone else to take the lead.

An entrepreneur has to be motivated and confident enough to take the initiative in business. If you answered **b** you may be looking for a mentor, if **c** then you could probably do with a lead partner.

2 Do you find yourself looking at ways of doing things and thinking 'I could do it better'?
   a All the time.
   b In my specialist field, yes.
   c Not really.

It's a characteristic of the entrepreneur that they are constantly assessing the efficiency of the operations around them and looking for opportunities to take something better to the market.

3 Do you have a lot of ideas?
   a Yes, I never stop thinking.
   b No, but I have one or two that I follow through on.
   c Not really, but I'm good at developing other people's ideas.

The entrepreneur has lots of ideas, even if not all are good, simply because they are constantly questioning. If you answered **b** you may be more an inventor than an entrepreneur, if **c** then you are probably a good team member but not necessarily ready to take the lead.

4   Can you make the most of a team?
     a   Yes, I love the buzz of a team when it 'clicks'.
     b   I prefer to work alone.
     c   I love working with my colleagues but shy away from setting the agenda.

A good entrepreneur knows how to make teams work for them; if you answered **b** and can't or won't work with others then you limit your own scope and therefore your ambitions. If you answered **c** then you need to think more about your role as a team player or team leader.

5   Are you afraid of risk?
     a   Nope, I don't think about it.
     b   Of course – everybody measures risks before making decisions.
     c   If I'm honest my fear of risk probably holds me back.

There's a fine line between recklessness and boldness, but overall the more you fear risk the less likely you are to be agile in making business decisions. The story of most successful entrepreneurs involves making snap decisions (and the right ones) despite the risks.

6   How do you feel about failure?
     a   It happens; I'll learn the lessons and move on.
     b   Certainly something to be avoided wherever possible.
     c   I would be mortified to fail at something.

Failure is part and parcel of business, so examine your attitudes. Having no fear at all may simply mean you haven't understood what's at stake but if you don't accept that there will be some failure at some point then you probably won't take your chances when they present themselves.

7   What are you prepared to sacrifice to get to where you want to go?
    a   Everything!
    b   My time and what funds I have available.
    c   Realistically, my family time is precious and I would never risk their financial stability.

You don't have to be prepared to throw everything away to make it but it's important now to understand your own limits before you find yourself up against them. There's no doubt that a driving ambition comes at a price in both time and money. What are you prepared to pay? Knowing your limits is essential.

8   Does your car have a name?
    a   No.
    b   No, though my first one did.
    c   Why yes, as it happens.

It might seem an odd question but if you can get even a little bit attached to an object like a car then you are probably going to be emotional about your business. Be aware of that tendency because it may affect your exit strategy when the time comes.

9   How organized are you?
    a   Totally.
    b   I get most things done I need to.
    c   I'm a creative genius, why would I need to be organized?

As well as self-confidence and drive you need to keep a grip on organization, whether that means your own personal schedule or that of your business(es). Don't think that this is some art form you can make up as you go, if you aren't disciplined enough to organize the smallest details then you'll need help from someone who is.

10 Do you think life is fair?
  a Irrelevant question – I make my own luck.
  b Largely, yes, life has been kind to me.
  c No, it's unjust.

We all get breaks, but the real entrepreneur makes their own luck. If you think life is fair then good on you; you're probably getting by just fine but may not be taking life by the horns. If you think life is fundamentally unfair then ask yourself if maybe you're accepting the agenda that others have created for you rather than setting your own.

OK, now that you know the attributes you need and are happy that you have enough of them to get going, let's think about the aims and objectives of an entrepreneur.

2

EXIT – IT'S IN LARGE LETTERS AND LIT UP FOR A REASON

I n daily life, just as in the Den, I see too many people with no long-term strategy for what (and when) they want to get out of their businesses.

It may sound counter-intuitive, even defeatist, to start a book about building businesses with a chapter called 'EXIT', but, bear with me, it does make sense. Entrepreneurs or venture capitalists, call us what you will, but basically we want out and so should you. We get our buzz out of analysing a business quickly, buying it, improving it or turning it round from loss to profit, and then selling it; that's what this book is about. Too many people get attached to businesses they have built up over time and fail to set an exit strategy. I should know; I've done it myself with a business that I am particularly fond of. I could have sold it for a lot of money some time ago but I didn't – it's too much fun running it and I really like the people in it. But it is the exception that proves the rule. In all other cases, my aim is to make money not necessarily when I own the business but when I sell it.

Damn, there is one more exception to the rule – land and property. Land and property assets in the UK and many other countries are a long-term one-way bet. OK, my portfolio of properties has lost a lot in value since the heady days of 2007, but as the saying goes, 'Land is a good investment, after all they're not making any more of it', and demand goes up with the increase in population. So I tend to keep property assets and since they are held in companies, I do have some that are long-term holds.

Let's get back to the point of having an exit strategy. Rule one of entrepreneurship is: before you buy or start a business make sure you've got a clear strategy of how, when, and to whom you could sell it. If you picture yourself owning something and showing it off, rather than picturing yourself going to the bank on the day you sell it on, then you're not an entrepreneur, you're a collector. So, at this stage in the book I am emphasizing the point of thinking through your exit strategy.

FAQ – Predicting the Future

Q: *How can I get an idea of the kind of person or company who might buy my business before I start?*

A: Fair point, you're never going to be 100% right about possibilities that are a few years down the line. The chances are you will sell it to a trade sale – selling it, for example, to a bigger business in the same industry as you. Think about who are the big or medium-sized players in your sector. Perhaps it will be a private equity investor, so think about them and what they are looking for. Work out where there is synergy between your products or markets and other companies or equity funds. You need to do this now for two reasons:

- because it may slightly change how you go about growing your business

- because it makes sure you have your eye firmly fixed on the goal of being a rich and successful entrepreneur.

I think many business people have an innate tendency to hold on to assets for too long rather than sell them for a profit. Let's start with the example of buying shares in publicly listed companies. I know some people who have made money out of selling shares early, even against their instincts; but I know a whole lot more who have made a loss because they sold too late or never got round to selling the shares at all. It's better to sell early and make a reasonable profit (even if the price is still rising) than sell late and make no money at all, particularly if you have a plan for how you will invest the original capital, plus the gain, into something else.

Rule one of entrepreneurship is: before you buy or start a business make sure you've got a clear strategy of how, when, and to whom you could sell it.

How many times have you heard people say 'Oh, I bought the share at the right time and it shot up but I didn't sell it and now it's on its way down. I still don't want to sell it because I'm sure it will recover and go back to the price it was at its peak.' Let's think about the logic, or rather the illogic, of that statement.

Start from the basics. To make money in shares is easy – buy shares when their price is low and sell them when it's high. When I say that to people they get very annoyed and frustrated. You may feel the same; it's a statement of the obvious and leads to the question – 'Yes, but how do you know what to buy and how do you know when to sell?' In fact, it's just possible that your frustration has made you throw this book against the wall; so I'll wait a moment for you to go and get it back before I explain.

Go back to the statement and put yourself into the position of the person making it. 'Oh, I bought the share at the right time and it shot up but I didn't sell it and now it's on its way down? I still don't want to sell it because I'm sure it will recover and go back to the price it was at its peak.' In the first place you've done well. You bought a share and it went shooting up, your timing was good. Why didn't you sell it? The only logical reason is that you thought the share was going to go further up. But is that logical? After all if a share goes up by 25%, what are the chances of it doing so again? Yes, there have been cases where it has but you're already looking at a great percentage profit so cash it in. We don't, of course, because of a heady cocktail of greed and inertia – it's so much easier to sit back and enjoy the ride than to step in and make a judgement call. If you want to deal in shares, then buy them when they are at a low price and sell them when they have gone up. If they have gone up, then as long as you've covered the broker fees, you win every time. If you hang on then you have the chance of losing.

The Eurotunnel linking the UK with France is a brilliant example of how we sometimes instinctively get this wrong. When the shares in Eurotunnel were first issued you could buy them for about £3. Within a year they had risen to £12. Many people didn't sell and subsequently they have fallen to almost zero. A mate of mine got the first dividend cheque for the £400 he had put in at the start of the Eurotunnel project years ago, and it was a cheque for 17 pence. Since he pays in cheques to his bank by sending them off to his branch in the mail, he would have been better off tearing the cheque up than buying the stamp needed to send it to the bank.

About three years ago I was discussing share-dealing strategies with a bloke who argued with my 'If it's gone up sell it' philosophy. His idea was different. He believed in buying some speculative shares into his portfolio and selling them when they had made a profit; he then transferred the gain he had made on those shares into solid dividend-paying shares that couldn't go wrong, like RBS and Lloyds Bank!

Again, like land and property assets, there is an exception to my rule. You can buy a share and keep it forever. Study the company carefully before you make such an important decision and then buy it for a very long-term hold. This is the Warren Buffet strategy and it has done him no harm.

Think about it; if a share goes down from 100 pence to 50, it has collapsed by 50%. In order to go back to 100 pence it has to rise by 100%.

The second part of the statement was, 'I still don't want to sell it because I'm sure it will recover and go back to the price it was at its peak.' This is equally fallacious. If a share goes down it is for a reason. The market, which has got a lot more time than you to study these matters, knows something that is making them take their profits or cut their losses. 'When a share goes down sell it', is another good rule of thumb. Think about it; if a share goes down from 100 pence to 50, it has collapsed by 50%. In order to go back to 100 pence it has to rise by 100%.

Tip from Shaf – If it Looks Too Good to be True, it Probably is

Businesses do sometimes make huge leaps forward, based perhaps on a single deal. But always examine any opportunity to make sure you understand the risks as well as the rewards. Get Rich Quick schemes look attractive because we all, from time to time, tire of the long, hard grind of making things work. We long for a sudden leg up in the world. Such schemes lure you in and then let you down. By the same logic, think carefully whether your enthusiasm for a new proposition is truly based on the realistic potential of that proposal, or whether you're allowing yourself to be seduced by the promise of an easy route out of the hard work.

Now let's take a couple of examples of the risk business again, starting with personal finance. People sometimes blunder into situations that have a very high risk, though they seem not to have known it. Take buying property abroad. There are Brits in Spain who bought properties that are now being repossessed because the developer who sold them the property didn't have the right to do it. It may be unusual, but there is always a risk of fraud. The fraud risk is made much higher if you're dealing in a foreign country where you only know enough of the language to order a couple of beers. You are completely dependent on advisers for whom English is not their first language and who make assumptions that you understand things that you do not.

Again, a lot of people retire to Spain. They have really enjoyed being on holiday there and retiring to the same place seems like being on holiday all the time. They sell up in the UK, buy a house in Spain and all looks well. They have their Old Age Pension from the British Government and their company or personal pensions that they saved up for all their lives, so there's no risk at all. What about currency? The pound has just plunged against the Euro and those people are in trouble. They can't afford their lifestyle with the new reduced pension. OK they'll move back to the UK. But everyone is trying to sell their house in Spain and it's in a British ghetto. The locals don't want to live there and the other Brits who might have bought it have learned from your mistake.

The point of being an entrepreneur is to buy companies for a low price and sell them for a higher one. The house in Spain example is one where people aren't thinking like a business but instead allowing their hearts to rule their minds on what they buy and where. This sounds fair enough because they want to live there. In reality we are all businesses and if we plough all of our assets into one proposal we become very exposed businesses. The idea of this book is not about being averse to risk but about weighing up risk. Those unlucky souls caught out in the Spanish property downturn probably didn't see themselves as taking a business decision, but they were, and did so without fully weighing the risks of currency devaluations.

Mind you, it's not just consumers who make stupid mistakes. Consider this story from an adman who became a serial entrepreneur. 'I sold my advertising agency to a big company in a deal that involved the big company buying three other agencies and putting them with mine into a group wholly owned by the big company. I had to agree to run the group for at least 3 years to earn the maximum sum in what is called my earn-out. The highest amount I could receive all together for my old company depended on increasing its profits in the 3 years to, let's call it, £x. When I started, I immediately, and fairly, transferred my salary from the profit and loss account of my old company to become a cost to the group. This immediately increased the earnings of my old company by my salary. This was a major contribution to the increase of £x I had to achieve and made the earn-out pretty straightforward. The managers in the big company didn't seem to realize that this is what would happen when we did the deal.'

I think such muddled thinking is common. Big companies are quite frequently mad, absolutely barking mad. It's often because the bonus system for managers is out of sync with the companies real interests; something that a small company must avoid if it is not to fail.

Just one more word about 'business nous' before we continue. If rule one can be said to be self belief, then rule two of entrepreneurship is to keep a clear head and, above all, believe the numbers. The big mistake a lot of people make is to look at business numbers and read what they want from them. If a new business opportunity really excites you emotionally, then be careful that you don't read into the numbers more growth or the potential for fewer problems than are actually there. If you're running a business and your information system tells you that your profit margin is trending downwards, then investigate it and do something about it. Do this when it is down by 0.5%; don't wait until the drop is at 10% or more.

Don't forget that 'exit strategy' is two words. It's not enough just to know when and how you are going to get out, you also have to let that shape your strategy. A lot of entrepreneurs don't make the most of their opportunity because they fail to see the impact of the exit strategy on the way they run the business. Take property developers. Developers buy a property that needs a lot of work on it. They do the work to make it sellable at a profit and then they sell it. Some do the work at the lowest possible cost to ensure that the property passes the assessment of a buyer's surveyor. Those are the ones who have remembered their exit point and based their business strategy firmly around it. A lot, however, just can't resist the temptation to do the property up to their own taste as though they were going to move into it. They spend much more than is necessary in order to produce a property of which they can justly be very proud. They still exit with money in hand but by seeing the way they exit as simply the end of the deal they haven't geared their business strategy in the best way to make maximum profit. The first group have business nous, the second don't. The first group have a clearly articulated and well-executed exit strategy, the second only have an exit.

Another important point to bear in mind at this early stage in your bid for glory is that it is never too early to start networking. When you come to implementing your exit strategy, the more businesses in your sector that you know and whose people you deal with the better. In fact, making contacts with business people

FAQ – Striving for Quality

Q: *Surely there's some room for me to have a passionate desire to make my product as good as I possibly can?*

A: Yes, I like people to feel passionately about their businesses, but not to the extent that their passion is reducing or completely removing their return on investment.

in your area and joining the various business-orientated clubs and forums that are available is something to do right at the start.

Business people talk, quite rightly, about setting objectives and communicating these to everyone involved in achieving them. It gives a clear focus and makes sure that every action that they take is aimed in the same direction.

Similarly, as an entrepreneur, you need an overall aiming point to guide your tactics and actions. That overall aiming point is the exit strategy and it's never too early to start thinking about it because it will guide and shape what you and your people will do now and in the future.

3

BUY THE RIGHT BUSINESSES

The problem is not finding the right business to buy, but finding the one that's right for you. There's no shortage of businesses on sale, but this is much more than simple horse-trading. The trick is not just to size them up and pick the healthy one (the best buy may be looking pretty shocking as a going concern right now). No, the trick is to start by taking a long hard look in the business mirror and deciding just what you can really bring to this particular company – what it is that you can add to a business that will transform it from a business either doing badly or doing so-so to a thriving enterprise that people can be proud to own and work in?

The successful entrepreneur quite quickly builds a portfolio of companies. I have my main companies, my property companies and investments in several others, some with a small percentage of the equity, some with a large one. As with the portfolio of most entrepreneurs you can detect a thread that connects most of them up in some way or other. I am happy, from time to time, to take on an opportunity in a totally new area of business where there is no connection with my current portfolio, but if I do that I generally want to get in and out as quickly as possible. I am more likely to be interested in longer-term opportunities where I can see one of my companies or one or more of my people being able to improve the situation in the target organization quite quickly. So this chapter is about spotting opportunities to buy the right company. Often, of course, the company I am thinking of buying is in trouble – that's probably what caught my eye in the first place – and I'll talk more about turnaround situations in Chapter 7.

Having identified the benefits that buying a company can bring to you and vice versa, the next problem is to work out how much you ought to pay for it, whether it's to buy the whole company or a part share in it. It's a big topic and you have to get to grips with a bit of financial theory, so let's get down to it.

Does the company fit?

In the business schools they call it 'looking for synergy.' Fundamentally, synergy comes where a new whole is greater than the sum of the parts; Business A buys Business B to create Business C. Business C is bigger and more successful than the two businesses were separately because a synergy between the two has made something good happen. Synergy is a good word to describe what I am seeking. I look for the nub of the opportunity in a new business and then look for synergy in various ways. The numbers are a good starting point, particularly if you look at the assets and liabilities that they reveal.

Assets are an opinion

I have made a lot of money out of buying businesses where the current owners were either underestimating the value of their assets or, more likely, overestimating the value of their assets. In the first case some owners do not think sufficiently outside the box to realize that their assets could be worth a lot more if they were combined with another customer database, for example, or enhanced with the addition of another line of products. If I can realize the potential of the undervalued assets, then it makes good business sense to buy them for a price that reflects their current owner's lower valuation. The seller is valuing their assets on a stand-alone basis; I am seeing them in the context of what I can make them worth if I bring the business into my portfolio.

The trick is to realize what the assets of two or more businesses will look like if you put them together. So in the case of a customer database, the seller sees their customer base as the ones on his customer file whilst I see it as that file plus one or two others that I control. I know that by adding it to my existing customer databases I can reach all those new people with a salesperson or an e-mail as soon as the deal is done.

> *The seller is valuing their assets on a stand-alone basis; I am seeing them in the context of what I can make them worth if I bring the business into my portfolio.*

A classic example of leveraging a database is what I advised Cheryl Hardwick, the managing director of www.boffer.co.uk, to do. Boffer is a deal-a-day site. It sells only one product per day, sourced from stock from bankrupt companies and excess stock. The bulk of the stock is sourced through another company I have an investment in called CPM Asset Management, a company that offers a very rapid way of turning problem stock into cash. CPM is headed up by another guy who I think is going places, Alfi Ariff.

Boffer has a tremendous cult following. It sometimes has in excess of 30,000 unique visitors per day. However, the fact that it only has one product on sale per day does restrict the possibility of ramping up the revenue. My advice to Cheryl was that she should set up a sister site to Boffer and leverage the Boffer database by encouraging Boffer customers to visit the new site. On 15th December 2009 the Boffer sister site www.bigoffers.co.uk

was born. Bigoffers also sells excess stock, again sourced from CPM asset management. But it has several thousand products on its website. On its first full day of trading it did 500 orders with no advertising apart from an email to the current Boffer database. That's the effect of leveraging a database.

The second case, overestimating the value of assets, often arises because the owners are being unrealistic about the effect of a change in market conditions; the current property market is a good case in point. People do not want to admit that the value of their house or their office (in this collapse particularly commercial property) has gone down along with the rest of the market. In the case of a house owner this need not be serious; they simply stay in the same house until things recover. In the case of the owner of a business such refusal to face facts can be dangerous.

Suppose I am looking at a business with assets that I think are worth £1,000,000 – half the unrealistic value that the owner puts on them. I offer, say, £900,000 and they reject it. Three months later I notice that the business is still for sale. I have another look and it is obvious that things have got worse and that the cash situation must be becoming serious. Do I repeat my offer of £900,000? No, this is getting close to what is known as a 'fire sale' and I go in much lower. If I have judged the precariousness of the owner's situation correctly I will get the business for that lower price and the owners have cost themselves a lot of money by forgetting that the value of an asset is an opinion, not a fact. They had an unrealistic view of the value of their assets.

Here's an old chestnut to make the point. A jobbing builder has, amongst other things, two assets on his balance sheet – a cement mixer he purchased last year and is now writing off, or depreciating, over 5 years and some bags of cement valued at their cost to him. His profits this year are only reduced by the depreciation on the cement mixer, 20% of its cost. This is very different from its value; indeed it is highly unlikely that second hand it is worth the balance sheet value.

Now go and look at the yard where the assets are kept. It so happens that an apprentice emptied the cement into the mixer, added water, was called away to do something else and by an oversight left the cement in the mixer over the weekend. It solidified, as cement tends to do, rendering the stock of cement unusable and the mixer unfit for its purpose. What now should be the impact of these assets on this year's profit and loss account? We know, and so does the builder, that the value on the balance sheet should be written off now, knocking a significant sum of money off the bottom line. But this brings profits below expectations and would upset the bank manager. So the builder wheels the mixer into a dark corner of the yard and everyone is happy. The value of an asset is an opinion.

Reality strikes only when the builder needs cement and a mixer; it will cost cash to hire a mixer and buy the raw materials. In the end cash is reality.

Now look deeper at the other assets and liabilities, using an example of a maintenance business I looked at. Their business was sending engineers out to repair heating and air conditioning systems on a regular or call-out basis. I was interested on behalf of another company that was in the installation side of heating and air conditioning. It seemed to make sense to combine the two companies, hoping that they would generate more business for each other from their existing customer bases. I looked at the assets of the maintenance company. These included quite a stock of spares with a fairly high book value. Now I know my limitations and valuing a warehouse full of air conditioning spare parts is not one of them.

I got the technical chap from the installation company to give them the once over. He reported that a lot of them were old and fit only for boilers and other installations that were quite old and probably needing to be replaced. So the book value of that asset was wrong. I then looked at quite a healthy sum of money in debtors – a lot of customers owed the company a lot of money. But that's not the end of it. I had to ask about the age of the debt. Have any of the companies on the debtors list gone bust or got into trouble? Essentially, what were the chances of getting anything like the value on the balance sheet into the company as cash? There were bad signs in this area as well, with an aged debt analysis showing that a number of the invoices were overdue and another number very overdue. We walked away from that one.

I could have taken the true value of the assets into account when I decided on the value of my offer for the business or I could have tied success in getting those debts into the contract. I could have made an offer contingent on how much of that debt actually became cash over a certain period of time; but what with the obsolete stock and everything else, walking away was the better plan.

Consider the liabilities too. I remember a managing director telling me that she had a large sum of money in creditors that had been there a long time because the supplier had let her down and not fulfilled their side of the bargain. I got on the phone to the suppler and found out that if he were paid cash immediately he would settle for 60% of the liability. This is not a job for shrinking violets. I kept that vital piece of information to myself. It affected what I now knew the business was worth, a bit more than it was when I, and of course the seller, took the tricky supplier situation into account. I hate to say it again, but I'm going to – assets and liabilities are opinion, cash is reality.

Other synergies

As well as the numbers, look at other aspects of a target business. Perhaps they use the same suppliers, sell to the same market or even the same customers. Perhaps you offer both companies a new channel to market. For example, would a link from your website to theirs increase sales and vice versa? Would it work to combine the two websites? www.boffer.co.uk and www.bigoffers. co.uk is an excellent example of this.

There is also something about having the expertise already on board that can make an opportunity seem right. Suppose you have built up skills in, for example, web selling and viral marketing. That could make a target business look attractive if it meant you could grow it using your existing skills.

How do you find out where these synergies lie? Well, you talk to the managing director and owner of the business of course; you research their website and perhaps talk to one of their customers. But don't forget the front line troops. Speak to the people who really know at the sharp end what the opportunities in the business are. Talk to the salespeople, for example; they'll almost certainly say things like, 'If we only had product B as well as product A we could do a lot more business.' Speak to the people doing the purchasing and you'll hear something like, 'We could almost certainly get a better deal on a number of items if we worked with a new supplier; but we are tied into our current supplier and senior management don't want to change.'

Cash is king

I am not sure if cash can be called an opportunity for synergy; but it's an important consideration in one company buying another.

Tip from Shaf – Supplier Loyalty

The worst answer to the question 'Why are we doing business with these people?' is: 'because we have been doing so for years and we have a good relationship with their people.' People have a huge inertia caused by their relationships with their current suppliers. Two lessons here:

- Don't let it happen to you. Make sure that all your suppliers are aware that you are consistently looking for cheaper ways of buying the products or getting the service.

- As a competitive supplier, look for opportunities to shake people out of their inertia by offering better terms. A taxi operator I know offered a perfectly good service from a town about 15 miles away from Heathrow taking business people to the airport. He got an appointment at a big company in the area and offered to undercut their current supplier. They were nice but used the 'long time … good relationship …' argument to turn him down. He went back to the company as the credit crunch started to bite and got the business.

Remember that buying businesses is a competitive situation. If you can see how you can improve the performance of a company and get a good return on your investment then so will other people.

It is unlikely that the target company will have any cash – that's usually why they're selling – so you will need some cash to fund the business once you have bought it. If you are buying from the administrators it is certain that the target company will have no cash. You also need cash for at least the deposit on the price you are going to pay the current owners for the business. Your source of cash is a combination of the cash you are keeping in your existing companies; don't forget that the owners of your businesses, including yourself, are on low wages to make this possible.

If you can see how you can improve the performance of a company and get a good return on your investment then so will other people.

Don't forget that you can use borrowings. Think about the situation – you want to buy a company but need to borrow a fair sum of money from your bank to do it. You rush out a business plan and get it down to your bankers. They drop everything and put a small team of people to evaluate the deal with the aim of giving you a decision within 24 hours. Oh, hold on a minute, that's not what the bankers do is it? In actual fact, at the end of the first 24 hours they will still be sucking air in through clenched teeth and slowly shaking their heads. If, eventually, they do think the proposition is a good one you're lucky; but they probably still have to get agreement from another two levels of management. Besides which, the banks right now are trying to repair the balance sheets that they wrecked with foolish gambling and they are being ever so canny about lending anything to anyone.

No, the trick is to have the money borrowed or otherwise sitting in a bank account ready for when an opportunity comes along. So, if you are borrowing to buy the new business, you are using money that you borrowed against another asset or as a facility for another business.

Here's an example of when cash in the bank was king. I got involved as one of a handful of bidders in the purchase of a business that turned over £4–5 million. A bit of wandering around and asking questions showed the main problems in the business were the prohibitive terms they had from their suppliers plus a route to market that had been replaced or enhanced by other and better routes by their competitors. I found out about the other four bidders and had a chat; I asked them 'What do you think of this business?' All four of them could see synergies with their current businesses and were very interested in buying it. I explained that I had proof of funding, a bank statement showing that I had the money in the bank to do the deal; I could act quickly. That night I found alternative suppliers that ensured that a huge improvement in profits would occur almost immediately. I then bought the business for a price that reflected current profitability and quite quickly sold it on to the other four bidders for a price that reflected the new profit picture going forward. That gave me a profit between the two deals of £250,000; not bad for a day's work.

Here's a story from a serial investor when we were talking about just such an issue.

I tried it and ...

I was interested in a start-up venture that had already secured some backing from another venture capitalist. Or so they said. Like you, I prefer to go straight to everyone else involved in a deal. When I picked up the phone to the other investor it turned out that they had been told I was already in, offering to invest. It seemed that the company was optimistically telling each of us that the other had already agreed to the deal. As it happened, we closed that loop by agreeing a different approach among the investors and going back to our optimists with the news that we now wanted a lot more control for the same money since we now had proof that they were chancing their luck. They took the offer and we did the deal – and if I'm totally honest I've always had a soft spot for their sheer cheek, but I can afford to since I have the controlling interest in how they behave from here on in.

Mind you it doesn't always go right even if you do spot a synergy that will improve a target company's position quickly. I once tried to buy a £6 million water company selling posh bottled water through Harrods. It was said to be the purest water in the world and came from the Highlands of Scotland. The directors of the company, however, stayed in or near London. They weren't hands on and I could see that the overheads were starting to increase rapidly. They were not getting the best prices for things like warehousing and logistics because they weren't on site often enough. This meant they had to borrow more money than was really necessary at fancy interest rates. The director's expenses at that company were also extraordinarily high; so all in all I knew I could make the company profitable at a stroke. I offered them £150,000, which they accepted, although a rival investor pipped me at the post, ironically because I was busy filming the *Dragons' Den* the day the deal went down.

Tip from Shaf – The Competitive Benefits of Synergy

This synergy business puts you not only in a better position than the person you are buying from because of the knowledge you have, it also puts you in a better position than rivals trying to buy the same business.

Here's a good win/win example of this: I was looking at the assets of a distribution company with revenues of £360,000. I knew that if I diverted a couple of my current distribution channels through that company's I could double its revenues immediately. I couldn't wait to tell the owners about that ... no, of course I didn't. I made a bid to the owners of £100,000. They were pleased with that offer and at a stroke it got rid of the people who were competing to buy the company, because they didn't know how the £100,000 price tag was justified – wonderful thing this synergy business.

Finding opportunities

If you find a synergy between two or more companies, you are in a powerful position. Businesses that are worth nothing to the rest of the world could be worth money to you. You can buy such businesses for a pound if you look. The trick is to set up a Google alert for 'gone into administration' and then act on it. I was in my office talking to a pal about this and he looked very doubtful. I went over to my computer and picked up my Google alerts. Eight companies had gone into administration just that day.

The thing is to be proactive. An administrator will only contact you if they are having problems selling a business, so for the best deals you have to make the moves. Build up a network of contacts in the firms that specialize in administration in your locality and then broaden it as much as you can. Remember, the faster they get the company, or bits of it, into new hands for cash the faster they start to draw higher fees.

Prior knowledge, or knowledge that you get from people with prior knowledge, is what gives you an edge. Take the market I know very well, the property market. First of all you need to work somewhere which is conducive to the sort of business you are in. Edinburgh, where I live, has a good lively market for properties in Edinburgh and all the towns and districts around it. It also deals with properties nationwide, particularly commercial properties. Sources of fresh information on who's doing what, what's for sale and who's looking to buy include rivals in the market who probably meet regularly. (In Edinburgh, property dealers tend to gather in the same place for coffee in the morning.) Once a group in the same business decides to trust you and realize that you will reciprocate where you can, they will actually give you information about what's happening. They will tell you about something they have heard about that they're not interested in, for whatever reason. The group also looks for opportunities for joint ventures to reduce risk and make the best use of available cash.

Then there are your suppliers – in my case solicitors, valuers, surveyors and so on. They are all rich sources of information when they know and trust you.

Whatever industry you are in, and as long you are looking for businesses to buy and sell, get involved with the other people – rivals, suppliers and customers – as much as you possibly can as early as you possibly can.

Realizing an opportunity

Back to cash: if you see a new opportunity, contact the administrator with proof of funding – the administrator is only interested if you have access to money, and very interested if you've got it in your back pocket. There is no hard and fast rule for what administrators want to look at, so make sure you have a detailed CV showing the businesses you have bought. They may be going through a process of due diligence, i.e. a very detailed look at the target company. Now, due diligence is all very well but it's an expensive process and if you're not lucky with the people concerned it can take an interminable amount of time. Work out what you can afford in time and money and walk away if it looks too restrictive, expensive or time consuming. Due diligence will certainly reveal some risks to the transaction. It pokes around for problems and then sort of pretends that it has found all the risks and can therefore conclude a risk-free deal at the correct price. No deal works like that: there are always things that will crop up only when you take the wheel of the new business.

Generally speaking I prefer to look at a deal more positively than due diligence. I would rather pay a lawyer to write a contract that covers me if the business is not exactly what the sellers made out. Take the one about the assets in debtors. It's probably quicker and more effective to challenge the owners than to poke around in the debtors file to try to work out what will turn into cash and what won't. So, if you make your price contingent on a certain percentage of the money coming in over a period of time then the owners have to decide the likely outcome. And in the end they probably know much more about the real position of the debtors than any accountant sniffing around the file for the first time.

So, if you make your price contingent on a certain percentage of the money coming in over a period of time the owners have to decide the likely outcome.

Be careful, there is a big difference between buying a company the day before it goes into administration and buying it the day after. If you buy it beforehand then you are buying the liabilities as well as the assets. You've got the debt, the leases and all the people to deal with. You might think that all of these things are best avoided. One place where you will almost certainly need your accountant is the tax positions of the company buying the target company and the target company itself. The chances are that you will be able to make use of the tax losses as well.

What is a business worth?
Into the *Dragons' Den* came a chap with a proposition to sell us 5% of his business for £20,000. I checked that he understood what that meant in terms of his current valuation of his business. He was well aware that it valued the business at £400,000. To be honest, some people who come in have not done the simple cal-

culation of working out that figure. If, as in this case, 5% of the business is worth £20,000 then the whole business is worth 20 times that. The revenues of the business were £7,500 in the past year and the profits zero, so how could that valuation possibly be right?

Funnily enough it might be ...

So, how do you value a business? I'm going to tackle this topic in three chunks.

- Valuing start-up companies and small businesses that have been trading for a while.
- Valuing publicly quoted companies. This is the bit of financial theory that helps to put the valuation of small companies into context.
- Valuing a company that you are thinking of buying.

Valuing start-up companies and small businesses that have been trading for a while

As a potential investor or buyer of a small company you're looking for situations where an injection of your money, product/market synergies and expertise gives the target company the opportunity to massively ramp up its business. Think of the shape of an ice hockey stick put on a graph. It goes fairly straight for quite a while and then suddenly takes a rapid upward close to vertical line. Investors want to invest at the point on that hockey stick graph where the business has the potential to turn the corner to rapid growth. This means that the value of the company is much more about its future than its past.

To understand how to value a business, start by thinking about what your house is worth and how you know that. You can value it in various ways: ask an estate agent, find out what a similar house in a similar location was sold for recently by asking the buyer or the seller, or go to a site like www.houseprices.co.uk and get a record of the house transactions in your neighbourhood. But you can't be sure, can you? The fact is that you cannot know the exact value of your house until you have sold it on the market.

That's what market value means – the price that someone has agreed to pay for a house, a sofa, a car or, of course, a business. So it's really the buyer who decides what a business is worth, based on what the seller is willing to accept for it.

So, how do you go about it? Think first about how you make a return on your investment. You can take a salary as a non-executive director; but that could be counter-productive as it reduces both profits and cash: that limits business growth.

You could take the money out as dividends. Over the medium term that might give you the return you are looking for. In order to pay a dividend a company needs two things, first profits over and above its overheads and taxes and secondly the cash to pay it. More likely as a small company investor you are looking to sell the business for many times the amount you invested, to someone who thinks that they can make profits grow even more, and perhaps that their return could come from dividends. However far in the future a small business might be from paying dividends, its ability to do so eventually has an impact on what it is worth right now.

To make a big profit on selling a business you need two things. Firstly, a huge growth in volume: it's called scalability. Look for the point at which the business will really take off in terms of sales and then profit.

That's why the business in the *Dragons' Den* with sales of only £7,500 might be worth £400,000; but the entrepreneur will have his work cut out to prove it. He has to make us believe that profit growth is close and very rapid, like an ice hockey stick graph. The value of a small or medium-sized business is governed to a certain extent by its current profits, but much more by its potential to grow those profits into the future.

Valuing publicly quoted companies

Let's go to the top end of company valuations, the value the stock market puts on the shares of a listed public company. This can be very volatile. If a number of people are selling blocks of shares in the same company, its share price may well go down. If lots of people want to buy shares the share price will go up. This changes the value of the company on a day-by-day, or actually minute-by-minute basis. That value is often called the capitalization of the company and is a simple calculation – the price of a share today multiplied by the number of shares. You can read that value in the financial pages of the newspapers.

Don't forget that the value people put on public companies listed on the stock exchange is just the same as an investor in small and medium-sized enterprises. It reflects investors' opinions of the ability of the company to grow profits, allowing them to pay dividends and increase those dividend payments in the future. It also reflects the speed at which that growth will arrive.

Remember that one of the best indicators of the value of your house was to look at what people paid for similar properties recently. So the best indication of the value of a company is to look at what recent investors paid for the shares. You get that too from the business pages.

So how does an investor use this information? Well, they know yesterday's share price and they can find out what profits, often called earnings, the company made in the last year from the company's website. Divide the share price by the earnings per share figure and you get a key ratio known as the Price/Earnings ratio, the P/E. Knowing how this calculation is made is useful; but investors don't have to do it for themselves because the journalists on the financial pages have done it for them. You can read the P/E on a daily basis in the papers or on numerous sites online.

So how does knowing the P/E help the investor to evaluate if a company has little or large prospects for growing its business and its profits? If the market believes that the company has steady growth prospects the P/E will be low; if the market expects the company to kick up a storm in the future the P/E will be high. So, a utility company could have a P/E as low as, say, 5 while the market might believe that a high-flying software company might look such an attractive growth prospect that shareholders will still buy the shares when the P/E is as high as, say, 40 – that is 40 times the profits that it made last year.

Now in the *Dragons' Den* we can get the information on one side of the P/E ratio by asking the person looking for investment what profits, if any, the company made last year. But we don't get the other side of the equation because nobody has bought shares in the company recently – there is no share price. So, that's what we are trying to assess when people are presenting to us. What is the company's real potential for growing profits? When is that growth likely to take place? This allows us to have a stab at calculating the P/E; a fair price for the share. After all, we are at the start of the chain of company growth that eventually produces the public limited companies of the future. Valuing a company is much easier if you can detect what experts, those folk in the City who are on first name terms with the captains of industry, think is its likely future performance. When you are buying a small company you are, of course, that expert.

With a small company the P/E is often referred to as the 'multiple'. This looks at last year's profits or next year's forecast profits and multiplies it by a number that reflects its prospects for growth. So, a would-be investor might offer a multiplier of 5 for a business with poor chances of growth or anything up to 60 and beyond if they feel the business is likely to take off. This is exactly the same principle as the P/E ratio.

Valuing a company that you are thinking of buying

If you can work out how much of your money and resources a business needs in order to turn the corner on the hockey stick curve, you have an indication of what your investment is likely to have to be. You also need to think through what value the current management will bring to the future value of the business. If, for example, they are pretty much inventors then you know that you will have to put in the vast majority of the management time needed to grow the firm. In that case you know that you want a considerable amount of the equity in the business, since it's really you, not them, who will make it fly. If you get the firm impression that all the management needs is the money to take the business to the next stage with very little input from yourself or your people, then you may well settle for quite a low minority interest in the business. The halfway mark for this is, of course, control. If you buy 51% of the business you are in formal control. If you own less than that, your control depends upon moving forward with the agreement of the majority shareholders.

So, put the transaction onto this spectrum and you have given the target business a nominal value; a P/E if you like. I say 'nominal' because if the business has not yet made any profits, by the

... if the business has not yet made any profits, by the price/earnings ratio method of valuation it's worth nothing. price/earnings ratio method of valuation it's worth nothing. If it's in administration it's definitely not worth anything and you may be able to buy it for £1. So how do you predict the future value of the business you are interested in buying? To be honest, a lot of it is instinctive, but if I can get at the nub of my opportunity or the target business's problems I can probably see a value that makes enough sense for me to make an offer.

Tip from Shaf – Getting a Feel for a Start-up Company

Start-ups, especially in the technology area, are very hard to value because they often have little or nothing in terms of assets or provable value, but their product could just be the next best thing. The DotCom boom and bust taught us the danger of that. One of the questions I like to ask is, what existing companies do you compare yourself with? Listen carefully to the answers. If they're based on solid information about the market then all well and good but if, as is so often the case, you start to hear that you're standing in front of 'the next Google', then ask yourself (and them) whether they're possibly more in love with the dream than with a realistic assessment of what they are capable of. They will obviously overestimate the value of their business as well.

If you want to be sure you have gathered all the data you need to make an analytical decision, here is a checklist of questions you need to be asking.

Product or service

- How does the company's products offer customers an improvement on what they have now?
- What do you think they will pay extra for that improvement?
- If the product is completely new, what new benefits will it bring to customers?
- What do you think they will pay for those benefits?
- What have the owners done in the area of patents or intellectual property rights? They may not have done much and that can add huge risk to the deal, particularly if it's quite easy for, say, a big company to replicate the product.

FAQ – How Do You Value Something Totally New?

Q: *I can see the need for due diligence, for calculating the numbers, and checking my facts, but I'm looking at investing in a totally new invention so there's nothing like it out there and no way of judging the potential market. Am I left with a leap of faith?*

A: Gut feeling is often what makes this game so exciting but you don't have to go it on your own and you'll often hear me asking entrepreneurs what market research they've done. You don't have to go to a big agency and commission huge surveys to do market research. Take this new idea and go to a handful of people you know and explain it to them. Then ask what they think and what they'd pay for it. This also has the advantage that they'll ask questions you hadn't thought of. If you can't answer all their questions, or you think you're not explaining the product well enough then you probably need more time to research it yourself. You'd be amazed how much quality feedback you can get for the price of a cup of coffee.

Market

- Who are the potential users of the product?
- How many people fall into that category? (Make sure it's a lot; you're an entrepreneur, you're looking for scalability.)
- What are the potential routes to market? Think widely about this, consider international markets, franchising, licensing, using the Internet and so on. Don't just think that their first idea is the only way to go.

Sales and costs

- What estimate can you make of their sales in the next two years?
- Check out the associated costs of producing the product or service.
- How will these numbers differ if you put money into the business? Make this estimate sensible not fanciful, but dare to be big.

Tip from Shaf – Evidence, Evidence and More Evidence

Prove the owners' assumptions in as many places as possible by asking for more detail. Ask the owners for a product endorsement from a potential big customer. Look at any customer contracts and Letters of Intent to validate the current owner's estimate of growth. If they say they've done some work on patents ask to see the documentation from the Patents Office. Think of every assertion the current owners are making and ask yourself how you can get them to prove or at least to show that they have thought it through. If you haven't got evidence ask for a postponement and work on getting it.

After you've done the numbers and looked at the evidence you should have a pretty good idea of the character and skills of the owners and their managers. Ask yourself:

- How well do they present themselves?
- Do they look confident or diffident?
- Can you imagine them in front of their main customers?
- Do they talk more about the market than their brilliant products?

If success in the new company is going to depend on the current owners, your assessment of them is as important or even more important than the figures you have used to value the business. This brings us neatly to the next chapter, 'Invest in People, Not in Products'. But before then, a quick tip for something to avoid when you're negotiating or even just considering buying a business.

Why give it away for a nice lunch?

A friend of mine is a business consultant and tells the story of how he learnt to keep his cards close to his chest when he was selling his services. He had done some work for the electronics division of a large multi-national and had been referred by his client there to another division; white goods. He spoke to the Managing Director of the division and got him interested in how he could help increase the efficiency of its distribution operation. The MD invited him to have lunch and brought in the Logistics Director. By the end of lunch the consultant had said enough for the Logistics Director to know where to look for the problems and how to find a solution. They had no need of the consultant. We call this giving it away for a glass of wine.

In another case, an excellent businessman but with no experience of buying companies was talking to the owner of a company that was in some trouble. Having had a look around he found the nub of the problem and explained it to the owner. At that point the owner had no need of the takeover and could go off and solve the problem for herself. It's surprisingly easy to do. When you have deduced a piece of information the other side does not have, perhaps to do with synergy between two companies, keep it to yourself until the negotiation is over: it's your information and it's worth money.

Now let's move to a topic which is much less precise than the numbers side of buying or running a business, and that's the people with all their attributes, skills, knowledge and eccentricities.

4
INVEST IN PEOPLE, NOT IN PRODUCTS

Truth be told, I invest in people rather than products. When it comes to businesses, I'm always telling people to look at the figures and believe the numbers but when it comes to people there's nothing quite like gut feeling.

To be a successful entrepreneur you have to be able to stand on your own two feet and trust your own judgement. You must make your own decisions even if they aren't the ones that other people would make, or indeed even if they are against the advice that other people are giving you. But that doesn't mean you have to do it all on your own. I'm a firm believer that if you don't know how to get the most out of working with other people then you're severely limiting your own ambitions. Since I'm certainly not a believer in limited ambitions this means hiring people and finding partners. The question is, out of all the people out there, how do you choose?

Can you recognize the differences as a company evolves?

The entrepreneur's experience of hiring and managing (we'll come to firing later) is a very different ballgame to the HR experience of an established company. When you first kick off with your start-up company at stage one, you're most likely going to be a one-man band with all the 'I don't need anyone' attitude that goes with such an adventure. Now, I'm not completely against that attitude; it's definitely cool to believe that you've got what it takes without other people being involved. I've certainly never for a moment regretted walking out of that office on my first day in a job to go it alone; but there's a difference between, as it were, needing people to lean on and knowing how to get people to help you to the next stage. Right from the start I looked for other people to work with, and I found them. Now I've got about 80 staff working for me. There is a big difference, however, in hiring when you start out, and hiring when you're relatively well known in the business scene. This is another example of what networking and getting involved in the local business scene from day one can do for you.

At stage one you might be struggling to get people to believe in you enough to join you. You're looking for risk takers who want to get in on the ground floor of a business knowing that it has little to offer them in the beginning save hard work, long hours and the odd sleepless night. They're out there and worth their weight in gold. They'll work for you until the enterprise is off and running then frequently they'll move on because they've done and learnt what they came for.

As time passes and your business becomes successful the problem is not getting people's attention and application forms; instead it's weeding out the ones you definitely don't want.

As an entrepreneur you'll find (I hope) that as you pick up momentum and start to thrive, all sorts of people will want to hitch themselves to your wagon. Some just want to be on a winning team, some find entrepreneurs more exciting to work for because the sky's the limit. Some will hope that some of the entrepreneurial attitude will rub off on them if they just hang around you enough. Which it can, to be honest, if they're making the effort to watch your methods and learn how you work. There can be a problem here because there are always a few dreamers who think that somehow teaming up with an entrepreneur is like getting in on the first days of Google or Microsoft. These people hope that they can become something just by being in the right place at the right time without putting in the effort or developing the skills. I think the real entrepreneur makes their own place and time; so I don't want that sort of person.

The first chapter should have helped you work out whether you are an entrepreneur who needs to be on their own or someone who needs a partner to make the most of their potential. If it's a partner you're in the market for, then the point about trusting them is at least as important as their actual skills. If you're a true entrepreneur, and I hope you are, then the early days are all about setting your own agenda and the last thing you need is someone else with authority pulling the reins in a different direction.

There's a huge difference, however, between getting on with someone down the pub or in a family environment and getting on with them at work.

When you're just getting going there are a number of options when it comes to taking people on. A lot of people tend to start by looking at the people nearest them. This usually means friends and family. That's fair, in that these are the people you trust and get on with and since those are my key criteria for hiring you might think they're the best bet for the job. There's a huge difference, however, between getting on with someone down the pub or in a family environment and getting on with them at work. Your relationship with friends and family is probably not one in which you take charge and they follow your lead, and your working relationship could strain your personal ones.

Instead, why not try talking to people, and a particular group of people at that? Your customers, or your potential customers, are a fantastic source of information. Talking to customers is something no business really does enough of. If you're just learning the ropes of a business you want to expand then talking to customers is worth every second. I started my first business on the basis of a conversation I had with a man on the train and I always swear that if you want the best business advice you will ask everyone you meet how their business is going, who is doing well, and why.

Soon enough names will start to come up in conversation as everyone who earns their salt notices the individuals who make a difference. I find it amazing that so many companies routinely pay money to agencies to interview strangers, calling it head-hunting and market research for example, but don't take the opportunity to get out in the marketplace and find out what's going on themselves. Getting out there doesn't have to be too time consuming either. Try to avoid getting in the car and doing too much travelling.

As you grow you will need people to work for you in senior positions because you can't have all the talents necessary in a big business yourself. If you're trying to do everything, you won't have the focus to drive the business forward and if you're a true entrepreneur that is your main purpose in life. When you get to that point you can accept a certain amount of authoritative people tugging in different directions. In fact, it can be healthy for the company as valuable input. It only works, however, if it's clear who is boss and who makes the final call. Fast-growing entrepreneurial companies are not democracies, or if they are they don't last long.

When you get to the stage where you can encourage your staff to come up with different ways of doing things you are clearly well established and confident in the people you've hired and have moved to the next stage of evolution.

Why get involved and stay involved?
Here's how I hire the kind of people I am keen to work with.

Firstly, I much prefer to do my own hiring so I try to put the time in to make that happen. There are a number of reasons for this. I often get a strong sense of whether the face fits the organization from the very first moment I meet the candidate. Even in *Dragons' Den* where I bang on about the numbers, I'm still basing a lot of my judgement on the person in front of me – on whether I could trust them, and whether I feel I could work with them. As the company grows you're also going to have to take into account whether this person is going to fit in and be able to work with the other team members and that's a much easier call to make if you yourself interviewed everyone in the first place. A lot of company MDs like to adopt a hands-off policy to hiring as a way of showing that they trust other people to make that call. I can see why they do that, but I suspect there's a bit of abdication rather than delegation there. In the end I expect everyone in my company to be working for me, so I like to make the call on whether to hire them. After all, it's your judgement that you are counting on to make your fortune.

Can you go with your gut, but not let it block out your brain?
All that is not to say that I'll take someone unsuitable for the job just because I like them; that would be stupid. When Darren Fenton made his pitch in the Den with his traffic control device (think of a blend of a torch and a Jedi light sabre), I couldn't see

why it would be a success since any rival with cheaper manufacturing could put him out of business. But I made no secret of the fact that I liked him and his attitude. I wasn't going to invest time and money in this idea of his but I have a feeling he'll come back to me and I would be happy to hear from him again. It's the same in hiring, you might like the person, but not for the role you are trying to fill at that time. That just means that you need to find a more appropriate place for them where they can really make a contribution. After all, your sort of people don't come by every day of the week.

I'll give you an example of the sort of thing I do at interview time. Rather than wade through conventional interviews where people tell me where they worked before and make up ludicrous answers to that question about 'What are their defects and weaknesses', I like to play it my way. I'll suddenly interrupt the conversation and give the candidate a simple challenge. I might give them a piece of paper, for example, and say 'make me a horse'.

Now I don't actually want a horse made out of paper. That's obvious – unless, of course, you're in a job interview when the tendency is to take very seriously what the interviewer says, particularly if the interviewer happens to own the company!

A surprising number of people respond as if I was famous for making my millions through origami. They apologize for not being able to make a horse, or worse they're reduced to silence because they just weren't expecting anything like that to happen.

What I'm looking for is how well they react to the unexpected, how they handle new challenges, and how creative they can be – and I don't mean at folding paper. The very best will come up with something that shows off their best side. That might be the will to have a go, or it might be a brilliant way to show me that I don't need a paper horse. (A good first reaction is to ask me why I want a paper horse ...) Any of these would be better than apologizing or staring blankly. Wrong-footing someone with a totally unexpected question can give you a lot of useful information about them. Watch their reactions carefully.

Do you need help hiring?

Obviously it gets harder and harder to take the time to interview everybody as the company grows. I still believe it's worth the effort, though, for every individual you hire. Think of it this way, you're counting on them personally to contribute and make a difference. Interviewing them in person is a powerful way of getting that message across; so do it for as long as is feasible. However, it's one of the many prices of success that the bigger you grow and the more activities you become involved in, the harder it is to find the time even for something as important as finding the right people.

So what are your options?

Outsourcing

A lot of companies outsource the whole issue and use third-party headhunters for their recruitment and I suppose sometimes they must be successful; but I have a problem with this option. The thing is that I rank gut feel and the question of trustworthiness above someone's qualifications for a job. I think that if you find the right person they'll be able to find their own feet and learn as they go. In fact to my mind one of the key criteria of the 'right' person is exactly that ability – to learn on the job. Third party recruitment companies, on the other hand, tend to value CVs, track record and paper qualifications above that gut feeling, precisely because they're not in a position to make that personal chemistry call on someone else's behalf. My people and I are much more likely to get the right people to join us.

Headhunters have two other flaws.

- They are very expensive. Not only that, but if you take the advice of this book and negotiate for everything it may not work with these particular people. Suppose you cut their commission down from 25% of first year salary of the person they place to say 15%, which is entirely possible, you end up with the awful feeling that you may not be getting a look at the best potential staff members because they are reserved for the people who pay full whack.
- By definition you do not have any first-hand knowledge of the candidates nor even reliable second-hand knowledge of the individual derived from a person who is 100% on your side.

Tip from Shaf – Managing Talent

Remember that while talented people are more difficult to manage than drones, it shouldn't put you off bringing on board obvious talent even though you may have difficulty controlling them. They can be the best contributors you can get. The best tip on managing talented employees is to give them as much responsibility as you can. Give them objectives of course, but let them break them down into the tasks needed to achieve them.

So if you decide not to outsource the process to a headhunter, then what can you do?

Use recommendations

Part of going with your gut is also learning to trust the judgement of others. Interviewing people on the basis of recommendations is a great idea. If you liked person A and they swear that person B is just the sort of person you need then it's probably worth taking a look at person B. But it's a risky process and you certainly can't go on a simple recommendation alone. Here's why ...

Remember that reference to evolution and the fact that your company will attract different people as it grows. Bear in mind what stage you are at when you're recruiting people. Someone who really helped you get a business going may not be so good at recommending a person to take over and run a going and thriving concern. If they tend to prefer people like themselves, and we all suffer from that a bit, then they'll recommend people who were ideal for when you started up. The same occurs when you have got someone who is good at running a going concern. They may not be so good at recommending someone to help you start up another business. One of the people I mentor made it work like this:

I tried it and ...

I took your advice about abandoning external headhunters and instead set up a recommendation scheme where my staff got a bonus if they suggested someone whom I eventually hired. I was a bit dubious at first, since I expected a lot of 'jobs for my pals' suggestions. To avoid that I put up a notice board and had people post their suggestions with reasons, so everyone else in the company could see who suggested whom. It worked well, sparked a lot of debate about who was good in the business, and reaped a fair crop of new staff.

I still think the best way of having that confidence is to have hired them all and for them all to see themselves as working for you, not for the company. That's why you need to be slightly wary of the recommendations approach. It can be a great way of finding rubies in the dust, but be very careful. Don't hire people who want to bring their old teams with them. Once you have that sort of set-up in the company you can get conflicting loyalties and even a whole company within a company. That's not how I like to run things. Since I'm most interested in building things up my way, and quite possibly selling and moving on, I can afford not to be too democratic about this. It really is my way or no way at all. That may make me sound

Don't hire people who want to bring their old teams with them. like a bit of a dragon (sorry!), but insisting on doing it your way doesn't mean you have to be a nasty person.

I've been known to get too attached to a company just because of the people in it – even to the point where I didn't sell the company when I knew I should have. That was probably a mistake but it's a hard one to regret. When you build an organization out of people you like and trust it is hard to let go of it – it's a bit like selling the family. If you get it right though there will be some people who follow you as you move from one venture to the next. That's not to say you need a personality cult of followers, but when you find like-minded folk and you reward their work with success don't be surprised if they want to be wherever you are and vice versa.

FAQ – Trusting Other People's Judgement

Q: *I've always gone on gut feeling for hiring and I've been let down badly by a number of individuals but I don't have anyone else whose judgement I trust enough to help me out; so any suggestions?*

A: The fact that you don't trust anyone else's judgement to help you might be revealing in itself. When you say you've gone on gut feeling are you sure you're looking for people you trust to do well for you, or are you actually just looking for people you like? Ask yourself where you've been let down in the past. If people have turned out to be incompetent then maybe you're giving too much weight to the gut feeling and not enough to doing your homework. Try the anonymous CV approach. Have someone strip out the names, sex and any other identifying content from the submitted CVs. Now just go through the raw qualifications and make up your short list on that alone. Finally when you come to make your judgement at least you know you're taking your pick from people with the right credentials.

Make sure your gut feeling is not blocking your brain.

Social networking

As I've said, once you start to grow your business the problem is more to do with weeding out the people you don't want than with attracting them in the first place.

Online recruiting works well, which is why it has exploded the way it has, but social media have until now been largely ignored for no reason that I can see except that it is different and people don't much like to alter the way they do things. That's starting to change, and it's no surprise because networks of people with common interests are the most obvious way of finding talent in any given area. That's one of the reasons why I invested in Vuru. co.uk – a social network for entrepreneurs and start-up companies in the UK. Once you have found the network that suits you it could easily become your main source of new possible employees.

Do you mentor your people and challenge them to maximize their contribution?

One of the hardest lessons I've learnt (some of my people say I still haven't got the hang of it) is not to micro-manage. I'm so used to doing everything my way that when an organization gets to a certain point it's a physical effort for me to leave it to the management to get on with things. That's one of the reasons I put so much emphasis on hiring. Knowing I've got the right people, and being there to choose them, makes it that much easier for me to be hands off when it comes to the running of the company. I trust them to do the right thing and I trust them to understand what it is I want from them. Beyond that, they know their own jobs better than me so I'm unlikely to be of any help if I meddle. Believe me, I really did get down into the detail asking why we had bought Bic pens instead of Staedtler, for example! Now I try to be much more hands-off.

A lot of entrepreneurs fall foul of the 'too much detail' hurdle though and end up bogged down in the management of companies they should be leaving to run themselves while they look for the next opportunity. Even the *Dragons' Den* investments that I'm mentoring add up to a lot for one person to keep an eye on, and since my intention is to keep moving and keep growing I need help with that. I've entered into a number of partnerships but the trick is to establish what the appropriate level of control and involvement is, and then create a structure that sets that in place. So for example with the *Dragons' Den* investments I teamed up with an Edinburgh-based corporate finance boutique, Tiger Advisers. I could never invest in everything that comes my way, but I don't like to miss out on a good thing when I see it so now I send them on to Tiger. Tiger sifts through them, raises the funding and grooms the businesses. Of course, to ensure that I retain the level of involvement that I want, I also take a stake in the spin-off company that Tiger have set up to own the shares in the companies they are investing in and I have a seat on the board. It means that I'm still involved in all the exciting bits of the business.

The recession has been good news in that respect. Jobs in the media, IT and the arts are drying up and so there's an army of highly talented and motivated professionals looking to establish new careers for themselves. So as well as coming to me with business opportunities they're also bringing themselves to the party. By seeding new businesses I'm in a great position to be my own talent scout and find the right people to help to develop existing and new businesses to move. When I started out I would never have expected to be in the business of running a talent school. But being a mentor is part and parcel of the entrepreneur's job. The best thing is that as all those individual investments in people are maturing, they have an uncanny habit of throwing up more opportunities for me to look at investing in. As soon as one person makes a business succeed, they find the next thing that they want to do. You should plan to do the same thing and get involved with budding entrepreneurs. Work with as many people as you can and spread your network wide.

Tip from Shaf – Don't Rely on the Facts

Investing in people is very much like investing in companies since both involve a mix of gut instinct and a careful reading of the facts. With a company the facts that count are the figures. With a person the facts are what you find on the CV. The difference is that a company's figures don't lie, and if they don't add up then it doesn't matter how much you like the look of it – walk away. With people, however, there is that certain magic of personality. A CV is essentially about someone's past and I'm looking to invest in their future. Just because someone hasn't done a certain job before doesn't mean they can't do it if you give them a chance. If you get a good enough feeling about someone then your belief in them can be enough to supercharge them and make them more able than they are already. The satisfaction of nurturing real talent is often as rewarding as turning around a struggling business or making a successful sale.

I'll be absolutely honest with you. I'm not in the business of running a large corporate over the long term. I'll seed new things for the future and I'll turn around struggling businesses but my preferred way of working is to move on to new pastures as soon as a good exit opportunity presents itself. So I don't worry about nurturing someone's career over several decades. When you've found the right people, keeping them should be a mixture of the job itself being what they want to do and the reward being right for their efforts. Get that right and people will work for you. It's not rocket science. Of course, I have my senior management team with whom I expect to work over the very long term.

I'd even go a bit further and say that some people shouldn't ever be made too comfortable – some should be encouraged to keep moving on. There are individuals who are only truly happy in start-up mode and too many start-ups have gone sour because bigger companies buy them and those companies have a different culture to the original. If you like being in there at the beginning of a company then get ready to bail out when the company starts to grow. Never let the grass grow under your feet. Jobs for life are history, so if you treat people right but they still want to move on to new things you can't stop them. Just keep an eye on what they do next. If you picked the right people and they move on you may find you want to buy into that next move.

How do you fire away?

You'll be a very lucky person indeed if you never have to fire someone. You can do everything right, take all the precautions you want and still find that either you don't get on with someone as you'd hoped, or else they can't do the job to your satisfaction, or some other factor comes along and wrong-foots you both so that the job changes for both of you. It is at this point that people seem to think that the entrepreneurial thing to do is point at them and say 'you're fired'. Now that might work just fine on a certain TV show, but in the real world that's a failure of the first order. Trust me; if I think someone isn't doing their job I'm not shy about letting them know the fact. But that's just it. You let them know about things. You get it out in the open and make it clear what is not working in your eyes. What you never ever do is fire someone who isn't expecting it. By the time you get around to firing someone it should be plain as day to everybody, especially the person concerned, that a firing is what's on the cards.

There are a number of reasons for this. Firstly there are the legalities.

It doesn't matter who you are. It doesn't matter if you're Lord Sugar, Donald Trump, or Shaf Rasul, the moment you employ someone in this country you're subject to UK employment laws, and they've changed a bit since the industrial revolution when mill owners effectively owned people.

Take legal advice before firing anyone because you don't want to waste the time, money and effort on a lawsuit or spend hours in a tribunal. The basics are that you have to start with a verbal warning, followed after a fair interval by a written warning, and then finally a letter of dismissal. There is simply no way you can just turn around and tell someone they're fired unless you have clear evidence of gross misconduct – but that would have to mean theft, assault, sexual harassment or worse. Even then you'd be well advised to get your facts sorted out before dismissing someone with all the accusation that gross misconduct implies.

Remember a verbal warning is a proper warning – along the lines of 'this isn't right, this is why it isn't right, and this is what I want to see done about it. Now consider this to be a warning and improve on your past performance or you're not doing your job properly.'

What it doesn't mean is snapping at someone or telling them they're rubbish.

Remember that, as well as following due process, this also gives you both the chance to work things out. It's possible that the other person has problems, or there are misunderstandings, and that they either need a bit of a jolt or some reason to come clean and start talking about it. It's also possible you've got the wrong end of the stick and some other factor is involved in the problem. Whatever the problem is, you can't just point to the door unless the offence is the sort of thing you'd want to call the police in for. Incidentally, that is almost certainly the better option if that's how bad things are.

Likewise, the written warning should be a considered thing. Ideally you've pointed out what's wrong in your verbal warning and laid down the ground rules for how that should change. If they still haven't changed then it's time to turn to the written warning, but you should have given the person concerned enough time to make the effort. If you've got an HR person then get them to take care of this whole process as they'll understand the implications better than you (they'd better, or else you need to look at getting rid of them too). The fact of simply handing it over to a professional shows greater due diligence and less whim at work. Certainly if you draw up a written warning have it looked over by a witness and keep a copy. Verbal warnings should be done in front of a witness where possible as well so you can prove that you followed the legal route.

Remember a verbal warning is a proper warning – along the lines of 'this isn't right, this is why it isn't right, and this is what I want to see done about it ...'

Having said all that, time is sometimes of the essence. If, for example, someone is being disruptive and causing problems with other people a swift break might be the right way forward even at the risk of a tribunal: it shouldn't be that expensive to get out from under even if you have to settle under the threat of a tribunal or even if you have to invest the cost in money and management time to actually go through a tribunal, although I certainly don't recommend that.

Minimize the pain – for everyone. If verbal and written warnings don't solve the problem then frankly sometimes there's nothing else for it and it's time to fire. There are a few ground rules for the actual act.

- Don't fire by email, fax, or sky-writer. Have the decency to do it face to face.
- Done right it should never come as a surprise but even so make 100% sure that they hear it first from you and not from anybody else unless you've handed the whole process over to an HR professional. Even then my own feeling is that if it is someone you hired then you should also be there to fire them face-to-face. If you can't do that then what are you hiding from?
- Don't tell people how sorry you feel for them. It's not likely to help them feel better and even if you mean it you run the risk of sounding like a hypocrite.
- Do keep to the facts. Keep it simple, keep it concise, don't dwell on failings but be 100% clear on those points that show the individual isn't doing the job satisfactorily.
- They always say don't do it on Friday as people then have the weekend to dwell on it but I'm not so sure about that. If that means they can spend time with their friends it's better than sitting alone at home the entire next weekday while everyone else goes to work.
- Have everything they can reasonably expect all ready – that means back pay, holiday pay, the lot. If there's a desk to be cleared then do it in advance – in most cases you don't want people going back in to the office for a number of reasons, including data security, morale and the fact that they can be tempted to sit there and stare out the window instead of moving on.
- Do have someone else there to act as a witness but whatever you do limit the embarrassment factor so don't do it in front of one of their close colleagues.
- Don't shout. Don't let it get personal.

- Don't let it drag on or turn into a debate. If you've followed the correct procedure this should be a mere formality for all concerned.
- If you're happy to help them with the next step then have references ready, or suggest options for them. Make sure they start to focus on their next option and not on you, or what might have been.

Anyway with a bit of luck, firing people will not be a big part of your business life. If you take on board the tips and methods talked about in this chapter you should get the right person much more often than not. If I had to sum my attitude up it would be:

- hire the best people you can get and can afford
- make sure you trust them and then dump them in at the deep end and watch them flourish.

I love it – watching a person blossom into a job they were not sure they could even do to begin with is a great pleasure.

We've looked at buying businesses and getting the right people in to help run them. It's time to talk about starting up a new business, and that's the next chapter.

5

START YOUR OWN BUSINESS

If it does not involve you buying a business, getting into business on your own means starting up your own business, and I'll talk about that in this chapter. But I'll also talk about the whys and wherefores of starting up further businesses to add to your portfolio once you have got going as an entrepreneur.

OK, so you've thought about going it alone and setting up your own business. Let's look at the basics of doing just that. First of all you need to start with a great idea. It doesn't have to be a completely new idea but it has to have the attributes of a workable new business. We'll look at that first. Then you almost certainly need some money and we'll look at sources of funds or seed capital. After that it's a question of building the business as fast as you can and developing it into something that someone wants to buy.

One thing to say before you even read the rest of this chapter: start saving now. You are going to need money for your idea and not to mention a few quid to keep body and soul together while the idea gains grip. So it's no pubs or clubs, don't buy the Manchester United or Rangers season ticket and tell your partner that presents are going to be very frugal for a while. Look, I've never said that life was easy. You are going to need money and the best and cheapest way to get it is to save it up.

What is a great idea?

Let's take a check here and think about the sorts of ideas that are attractive to customers and to investors. Notice that it needs to be attractive to investors as well as customers because you may be busy starting up a business, but you're already thinking about how to sell it on and get out. What is a great business idea? Here's what a great idea looks like and here's how you might come up with one. Using a couple of examples, I'll explain the process of having and evaluating a business idea.

Start with an overview – a successful business idea is one that meets customers' needs better than they're met elsewhere. It doesn't have to offer something completely new, it just has to have an element that makes people think: 'That's a good idea, I'll try it.'

Evaluating ideas

Now, be careful here. People who think primarily in terms of a great product are probably inventors or designers. Entrepreneurs, in contrast, think primarily about the market. Who will buy this idea, why, and what is the best way of presenting it to them?

A very common way of finding your big idea is to find it in your everyday life and in discussion with the people you associate with. Here's a good example of this:

A thirty-something woman had three children. This made her very aware of what children's needs and demands were. They wanted, for example, all the toys that they saw advertised and all the others that their friends had. They nagged hard to get them and when they finally got them, they would lose interest in them, ofter after a very short time indeed. She heard other mothers saying exactly the same thing.

The children wanted special toys at party time, so that their friends could join in an out-of-the-ordinary game for the duration of the party – there were bouncy castles for this purpose but that was about all. It was expensive to buy something for use on one day only.

People who think primarily in terms of a great product are probably inventors or designers.

She remembered that she really liked to give her first kid new, shiny toys straight from the toyshop; but she also remembered that her second and third children were actually just as happy with the hand me downs they got from their elder siblings, though not for everything. They had to have some things that were new, but for major items, like a tricycle, hand me downs were just fine. Her children grew out of toys; for example, the car, so joyously unwrapped, only lasted for 6 months before the kid couldn't get into it. She had the germ of the idea – a toy hire shop that would specialize in larger toys so that mothers could join a club and then hire the toy for the birthday party or whatever. She knew the pitfalls as well. Mothers would not like it if there was any dirt or remains of chocolate on the toys they were hiring, so she made the necessary arrangements to clean them thoroughly between hires. She would offer to hire out toys from a shop as well as a catalogue and web site. She got another mother interested and the two of them started to evaluate the idea. They knew the market inside out because they were the market.

Another common way of finding your big idea is to take an idea that is successful in one culture, overseas perhaps, and import it, suitably tailored, for the new location.

An example of this is Coffee Republic, a major chain of coffee shops started by the brother and sister team of Sahar and Bobby Hashemi. Sahar was used to the products and service she could get when she was in New York and missed them when she was in

England. In fact she missed the skinny cappuccinos and fat-free muffins so much that she knew that there had to be a market for them. She knew that other people would love them if they were introduced to them – and the rest is the history of Coffee Republic.

Now evaluate the idea strategically by considering the following questions.

Why has no one done it before in the geographical location that you have in mind?

This is most important for premises-based businesses – businesses where the customer comes on to your premises. Perhaps this is another reason why in the current climate I tend towards web-based businesses so that by using a countrywide delivery system the location of your stock and of your customers is nearly immaterial.

I have seen many examples of new businesspeople who believe that they can 'create a local market' by changing the habits that the local people have built up over years and make them spend their money differently. I get concerned when someone says 'There's got to be a market for it here, the nearest competitor is miles away.' It makes me ask why no one else has done it here. How can you be the first person to think that this idea will work in this location? Strange as it may seem, I'm more comfortable when there are outlets with a pretty similar idea to yours operating nearby. OK, probably having a competitor next door is a little close, but if they're miles away, perhaps the market is too. Starting a business is enough of a struggle without having to introduce a totally new concept to a sceptical local market.

This was a risk for the woman with the toy hire shop idea. She knew they had implemented the concept in New Zealand but there was nothing like it in the UK, not for the market she had in mind, reasonably well-off professional middle class families. There was nowhere in the whole country, let alone the town where she was thinking of setting it up. In investment terms I think this raises the first alarm bell. OK, this is an imported idea proven abroad; but does she need to take the risk of starting off with premises? Premises are very expensive and they siphon off all of the capital you have available to put into the business. An investor may think, 'Well I'll stay away from this one until she really has proved that sales from the shop make the shop worthwhile.' If she starts off just with the website and catalogue, she saves a lot of money and proves the idea countrywide without the premises risk. All she needs is a garage somewhere to keep the stock; it doesn't need to be smartened up to the standard for customers to visit.

FAQ – Using Only the Web

Q: *It seems unlikely to me that you can build a retail business without any premises if the customers are members of the public. Can you really do it by the web only?*

A: There are so many examples of this from eBay to loads of the businesses I have an interest in. It's a special kind of marketing though, so make sure you have the expertise to make it work, from web design to web marketing and viral marketing. Get it on board or buy it in temporarily. Don't forget that you still have access to normal advertising methods such as press advertising or even TV advertising. The fact that you don't need customer-friendly premises saves a lot of money you can then spend on fliers, promotions and other types of marketing campaigns.

Is it expandable?

We're not here to get bogged down in running a business that's only suitable for a very limited market. The toy hire shop scored well on this one, the owners even had ideas for franchising the idea as well as opening up more outlets. I like that; the moment you mention franchising and licensing an investor gets more interested, since it means attracting more investment-minded people and bringing in more capital into the business without selling shares in the main company.

To be honest with you I think that investing in business-to-business products that require a lot of technical skill and know-how tend to take a much longer time to make real money than a product that you sell in bulk to consumers. A really clever bit of software that does something new in the world of controlling and managing a big business is hard to get off the ground and harder to make money out of. There's going to be a lot more time and money put into supporting, getting the bugs out and developing the software for literally years and years before the return becomes massive. Compare that with building a simple concept on the web that has a potential market of all the adult consumers in the country or the world and there's no contest.

Expandability normally involves consumers.

Have you checked that it's not just you that thinks the need is urgent?

Some people have a passion for some very peculiar things. When they try to turn this passion into a business they find that few people share the passion. Don't get me wrong, I want you to be passionate about the idea and how popular it's likely to be; but don't get carried away. I know you're excited about taking your new concept to market and bursting for people to love your products and services as much as you hoped they would. But, whatever your motivation for getting into this, it's time to remind yourself about the real motive for going into business – making money. OK, OK, I know you want to have fun running your own thing; but believe me, there's no fun in running a business that's not making money. As the General Motors Executive so neatly put it, 'We're in the business of making money not cars.' So if you enjoyed your holiday in Egypt and got the hang of sitting in cafes where everyone smoked hubble-bubble pipes and drank strong coffee, remind yourself that smoking is so out of fashion in the UK that they're going eventually to ban it in all public places – even outdoors. This means that setting up the hubble-bubble concept in Central Glasgow is probably a very long shot.

Try not to get into a position where you're trying to push water uphill by choosing an idea that you love but that you're going to have trouble persuading other people to spend their money on. I don't mean to suggest that you should ignore intuition and passion. What I'm saying is that you should tune your intuition not to think about innovation in product terms, or in terms of a new market; but tune it to think about the link between the product and the market. Keep asking yourself: 'What is my strategy? What am I trying to sell and who am I trying to sell it to?'

The secret for getting feedback and working out whether yours is a great idea, in my experience, is to listen patiently to everyone who wants to tell you why your new business idea is rubbish. Fix a Cheshire Cat grin to your face and thank them for their opinion. Then run crying to your secret place and work out in private whether in their bluntness they've thought of something you've missed.

Crucially, you've got to ask yourself what is the underlying reason why a particular individual has offered their opinion of the idea in the first place – there's more politics to this than an Election campaign. For example: current work mates will be envious of your upstart ideas and damn them with faint praise, close family will worry that you're consigning them to Lidl and public transport for the foreseeable future. Friends will tell you what you want to hear and parents will wonder if you're going to waste the money they spent on your education after all. Funnily enough, it's often complete strangers who offer the healthiest advice; like the bloke in the pub whose mate had the same idea or the mini-cab driver whose insightful comment convinces you he's a moonlighting Harvard professor studying the start-up turmoils of British entrepreneurs. So passion is for people starting business but not really for investors.

There's normally at least a grain of truth in most advice that will be dished out in your direction. The key is to pick those grains from the sludge of disdain, jealously, envy, worry, or fear that will inevitably surround them. Once you've done that you can start to see if your original idea still stacks up and is as viable as you first thought. Take your time over this. Changing your mind at this stage and admitting your idea was weaker than a homeopathic hangover cure will cause you some mild irritation as the 'I told you so' looks and comments come your way, but at least you'll still have a roof over your head and a credit rating. Plus you won't have failed. But you won't have succeeded either.

Has the great idea passed all the tests?

If your great idea has passed all the tests involved in the questions in this section, it's time to think about how to implement it. You need to think about, and eventually write down at least in summary form, an overall implementation plan. Start from the overall strategy for the new business and consider the following points.

- What products are you going to sell into what markets? This is key. Until you understand the product and the market you are aiming at you are still thinking in loose terms about the great idea.
- Since most great ideas start from making something or buying something in, you're also going to have to think about getting some cash into the business – you need to think about loan capital and share capital.
- Once you thoroughly understand the direction of the business and where its seed capital is coming from it's time to think about how you build and grow the enterprise.
- Finally, in this overview of an implementation plan you need to think about spreading the word of your business and how attractive it's likely to become to investors.

Product/markets

So your plan is at the stage of identifying your product and your market and finding the start up money to attack it.

Let's talk about markets and marketing. To be successful you have got to get so far inside the heads of your customers that you know not only what they need and want now, but also what they're going to need and want next year. So, back to your developing plan – describe and perhaps write down a detailed description of the type of customer you are going to appeal to with your new business. What is their background, what do they do, what papers do they read and so on? Get out there and talk to them, not only about your idea but also about their general aspirations and desires. Read the magazines they read and look at the adverts in them – they're a good clue as to how marketing people think businesses should address this market.

Think of it this way. There is no such thing as a product without a market, just as there is no such thing as a market if you do not have a product for it. So, think in terms of 'product markets'.

When you have been on your own for a while you will be surprised how many people are thinking of doing the same as you; leaving the big company and going out on their own. They will speak to you about their ideas and ask for your comments. Usually they take what I believe is the wrong approach. They have, for example, thought of or developed a new 'product'. It's an innovative idea for, say, selling educational aids – a package of training aids and books that they used to teach themselves how to appreciate grand opera, a 'starter's pack' for someone who wants to enjoy opera but hasn't a clue how to start to study it and learn about it. They have computerized it and think that with a bit of investment and work, that it could become marketable. And they could be right.

To be successful you have got to get so far inside the heads of your customers that you know not only what they need and want now, but also what they're going to need and want next year.

Unfortunately, this gives them a product but not a product market. They do not have a product market until they have a customer. So this becomes my advice. The moment you have thought of a product identify the market for it and think in terms of the product/market.

There's another way of doing it; start with the market. Look at a market or group of people that you know and understand. Perhaps it's the managers and people you have been dealing with for years in the big company. Think of their passions and hobbies, their general needs and wants, at work and at play. After all you know them well, so you know their bitches and grievances as well as their wants and aspirations. Now think of a product or a service that you think they would buy. If you can, think of another one and another one until you can see how you could generate a series of products to meet the demands of this market.

Right, let's recap for a moment.

- You've started to save money to put into the new business.
- You've got a vision of the lifestyle that you would prefer to the one you have now.
- You've assessed the implications of things not going well and decided to take the risk.
- You've thought about the position your business will have in the market and what will distinguish it from its competitors now and in the future.
- You have a clear idea of the market you're going to address and done some overall research on it.

Now you need a bit of cash ...

How do you get seed capital?

Can you still make a million when there's a recession on? You bet you can. Bank finance may be in short supply but there are lots of great low-cost business opportunities out there – especially on the Internet – that do not need a lot of seed capital, and it's still possible to get money if you look in the right places.

Go back to the key commercial considerations you need to take into account in setting up a new business.

- Do you have an idea that will appeal to a market that you can define and then reach?
- Do you feel passionately about that idea and the fact that you can do a better job than the people already serving that market?

- Are you prepared to work extraordinarily hard to get the business started and thriving?
- Have you got or can you get the skills and experience for the actual job you are going to have to do?
- Can you get the funds necessary to start up the business?

In the case of the first four points, whether the country is booming or busting makes no difference to your answer. The last point seems more problematical. With a credit crunch, the banks are licking their wounds and sulking in their tent, refusing to lend money even to people with good ideas. But you can get round that. There are other ways of raising finance than impressing a sceptical, and frightened, bank manager of the merit of your idea. After all, when interests rates are as low as they are right now, your friends and family will be keener than before to back a business that has a reasonable chance of giving them a much higher return. I'll come back to that later.

Capital comes into a business in the first place as share capital and/or loan capital. When you are in a job and planning to go on your own, save as hard as you can in the weeks and months before you take the plunge so that you have got a reasonable amount of cash to put in yourself. Ask an accountant how to put it in. For example, suppose you have £10,000; do you put it all in as share capital or as £100 share capital and £9,900 loan capital? My leaning is towards the latter, so that if you are able to take that money out later it's easier to repay a loan than muck about with buying back shares or releasing share capital.

So, really, my advice is: 'Try to find loan capital'.

Understanding bankers and getting loan capital

I believe that starting a business in a recession is perfectly possible and, funnily enough, offers opportunities that the good times don't. There is, however, undeniably one big problem at times like these – during a credit crunch it is very difficult to borrow money from banks.

Take time out for a moment to make sure you understand where financial lenders are coming from. If someone offered to lend you £10 for a week, but asked you to agree to pay back twice that amount at the end of the week, you wouldn't need to have read this book to realize that that's a very bad deal. Suppose, however, that you are completely broke and know that you will have £121 cash in benefits payment by the day on which you have to make the capital and 100% interest repayment – still not interested? Ah, I forgot to mention that your two children haven't eaten properly for 36 hours and that they're wailing for food. In such circumstances the loan sharks of the inner city estates make such loans, and prosper. This is a good starting point for considering the purveyors of loan capital. They're all like that; only the ones in banks are better dressed and less physically threatening. They are as dangerous to deal with as Old Nick, so don't sell them your soul. This is particularly true right now because they have so mismanaged their businesses that they have destroyed all the profits they had accrued over the last 20 years; they lost the lot. In the end, after the Government has pulled out, the main people who will have repaired that balance sheet disaster will be bank customers.

A bank's view is that they tailor their interest charges to protect themselves against the risk of default. The more difficult the situation the borrower is in, the higher the risk and therefore the higher the price of help.

If you are running a huge conglomerate and wish to borrow $250 million to buy up a subsidiary in another country, you will be wined and dined by various moneylenders eager to get your business at, perhaps, less than 1% above the rate at which the banks themselves borrow money. If you need £20,000 to tide your corner shop over a refurbishment, you will probably have to trawl the High Street to find a lender willing to lend you the money at 5% or 6% above bank rate. And they will probably want you to back the security of the loan by re-mortgaging your house; or leaving your kids with them as hostages (I may have made that last bit up but it's only a matter of time). Banks are indeed the people who lend umbrellas to small businesses only when it isn't raining.

Tip from Shaf – Finding Finance

You can avoid borrowing from a bank to start up your new venture by using other sources of funds. There are, for example, lots of deals out there for interest-free credit cards that could just possibly give you the bit of credit you need to get going. Suppose you need some computer hardware or software to start your computer-aided design company. Buy it on one of your current credit cards. Now transfer the debt to a new credit card that is offering at least 6-months interest-free credit on transfers. You should be able to buy whatever else you need using the 12-month interest-free offer the card is also offering on purchases.

If you can't pay it off at the end of the interest-free period you may well be able to transfer to another card. Word of warning though, keep a tight grip on when the interest-free period ends and work out well in advance what to do next; but if you are confident in your cash flow and it shows you will not have to pay the punitive interest on a credit card for very long, then that could be a way to go.
Current interest rates on credit card balances are more than 16%, so don't get caught. After all, that's why the banks make these 'generous' offers – careless people get trapped in a high-interest transaction that could cost them their business – always remember the 'bankers' on the inner city estates.

Finding share capital

If necessary, however, you may find yourself looking for share capital. You can find various sources of share capital but make sure you're happy to live with the results of selling part of your company to someone else. A bit like your previous employer, they're trying to make money out of your skills and hard work – personally I never wanted to give any of my main business away.

However, it may suit you to go this way, so look for other investors.

A private source, such as your parents, friends and family

This can be a good source but does have a downside if things don't go entirely according to plan. Letting down professional investors who understood the risks they were taking is much easier to deal with than letting down the family and pals you will continue to live with after the event. It's probably best only to take investment from people who can afford to lose what they are putting in. Don't just look at these people solely as a source of share capital. If they put money in they are involved in the business, so get them to put some time into it. If you are decorating new premises, they can probably help out with a paintbrush: there can be a thousand ways that someone who is motivated to help you get your business going can make a contribution. Final try: you don't have to put money from this source in as share capital. See if you can get them to lend the money for a fixed interest payment.

Letting down professional investors who understood the risks they were taking is much easier to deal with than letting down the family and pals you will continue to live with after the event.

I tried it and ...

I approached my family and friends and got no interest when I looked for one investor. When I broke it up into small packages and invited them to form a sort of club that I would give a little report to from time to time they got more enthusiastic. I got the money as a loan and the company is now 3 years old and doing quite well. I offered to pay them all back but they had got involved with the business and wanted to turn their loans into share capital. It means my giving away about 5% of the business but that seems a fair deal since without them I couldn't have got started.

A public source such as a business 'angel'

Angels are professional investors who make small investments in new businesses. The tax breaks such angels get reduces their risk hugely, and multiplies their returns. The upside of this source can include getting the benefit of their advice because most of them have accumulated their own wealth by growing their own businesses. The potential downside is that they will interfere and if they don't agree with your unfolding strategy this can be a problem. It's difficult to be a pioneer doing your own thing if you've got a parrot on your shoulder telling you how they would do it.

Venture capital funds

These are professional investors who build up a fund using money from many personal and institutional sources and invest it in a portfolio of start-up and emerging businesses. This has the effect of spreading investors' risk. Mind you, the success rate with venture capital funded businesses is not high. The fund managers only expect a few in ten to really fly. But they expect to make a princely return on the few that make it. Watch these guys though; they will try to get a massive amount of your business for as little as they can get away with. They also interfere using a light touch when things are going well and this may be an advantage, but is not so helpful when things are not going according to plan. In fact they can make matters worse if you are struggling a bit, by insisting on getting a consultant's or accountant's report which, of course, your business has to pay for. Venture capitalists generally avoid investing in completely new businesses, so you might have to get started before you can get them interested.

The secret when launching a business is to keep costs low and make every penny a prisoner. And there is no better time to do that than when times are tough and the recession is in the headlines every day. Negotiate for everything – remember that landlords lose a year's profit if their premises are vacant for 3 months; so they're willing to do deals. And so it goes on, you can really clamp down on costs when everyone is facing the prospect of doing less business.

One more thing when you are getting a business going; avoid the super car trap. I know it might sound a bit rich coming from a man who gets through Aston Martins faster than shoes but leave buying the Ferrari until you're officially on the rich list and at all times keep your feet firmly on the ground.

What do you have to do to build your business?

Before you accuse me of taking too much time to talk about selling and marketing, remember this – most new and small businesses fail because they don't sell enough. You may have the best customer service in your product/market; you may have the best people doing your selling; you may have a highly professional, user-friendly website, but if you don't keep up with the way your market is changing eventually you will stop selling enough. So here is the key to keep your business selling.

Prospect continuously

Most of us have a background from one part of the business world before we start up a new business. We come from production, sales, finance or wherever and this dictates some of the emphasis that we put into the business. One of the advantages of coming with a sales background is a complete understanding of the disciplines of prospecting. Salespeople know that when you are selling you are not delivering and earning revenue, and when you are delivering and earning revenue you are not selling. It is easy to let your start-up business reflect this in a cycle of selling activity and then delivering activity. It's easy, but dangerous. A hole in the order book now is a hole in the cash flow in about two months' time. This delay can give you a false sense of security, especially when you are busy delivering and find it hard to fit what needs to be done in the delivery side of the business, let alone add selling time.

But that is what you must do. Set aside at least an hour each week for prospecting – finding new clients – or more if your business demands it. During this hour make your phone calls or send out your mailshots or devise your new brilliant gimmicks for generating potential customers. Never, ever miss it out. Some people always do it on a Monday morning since that tends to be the time that other salespeople are in their weekly meetings or touching base with their offices or whatever. Don't waste prospecting effort. If you send out a mail shot and you are in a business where you need to follow up with a phone call, i.e. most businesses, don't send a huge number out at the same time. Send out just enough so that you have sufficient prospects to ring to fulfil your prospecting quota. This drip feed technique has the added advantage that you have to go back to it on a regular basis, thus automatically putting the hour-a-week discipline in place. Potential investors will always ask a question about the number of new customers you have picked up in the recent past and be unimpressed if it's none, or not enough to replace customers you have lost.

> ## Tip from Shaf – Build by Acquisition
>
> This may seem a bit fanciful if you've just started your business, but there is a most critical time in the life of a start-up which happens between 1 and 1½ years' trading. Think hard about that period; it is probably the worst time for start-ups to go bust. Two tips from this. The first is to plan for how you are going to get your business to defy the odds and secondly, once you've done that, look for small businesses of about that age that are in trouble – you can probably buy them for a song.

Big it up

Small companies face the challenge all the time of trying to look bigger than they are. They are trying to minimize the risk that customers and suppliers might suspect and be put off by if they think you are very small. Use all the normal devices ...

- Have all your meetings on your customers' premises. It's terrific; you drink their coffee and possibly get lunch as well.
- When they are coming to your location, arrange to be at a hotel – either in the lobby or in the restaurant.
- Use phone forwarding so that you keep in touch. I find it quite witty to be talking to a customer who has phoned a number in Scotland while actually I am cooling my tootsies in a swimming pool in Dubai.

- Don't stint on letterhead and design on the documents you send out. If your stationery looks as though it was produced on a children's printing press it is screaming 'sole trader' and 'only recently started'.
- Publish a newsletter or refer your customers and prospects to one on a web page. It takes time and you have to work hard at it so that it does not become actually or perceptively out of date; people will not read a company description on a website that looks as though it has not been updated for a year or more.

Get everyone to talk to customers regularly

The way to keep every member of your staff in touch with reality is to allow very few of them to be completely unexposed to customers. You can do this individually by insisting that your product developer attends customer progress meetings, for example, or en masse by inviting customers to come and speak at the annual company get together. I have seen web designers, for example, completely transform the way they think about their work when they come to have a real insight into what the customers are trying to do, and how they examine your web site to look at your offerings.

Speak to the press

The trade press, and indeed the national press, is always looking for stories. They have a lot of white space to fill regularly. Feed them what you can. Study the trade press and get to know the journalists. Eventually they will start to ask you for comments on stories they have got from an alternative source. This gives you a profile outside your organization and is good for improving your 'gravitas'. There is no such thing as bad publicity. To my knowledge, and astonishment, a mention in the newspapers, tabloid or broadsheet, impresses a lot of people. They just like reading a name they know – yours or your company's.

I put down one of the successes of the website Boffer to their relationship with the press. They are forever getting a mention in one or another newspaper or publication.

And, of course, there is your business and social networking to keep up. The more people who know what your business does the more leads you will get and the bigger you will look.

Be careful; go through the bureaucratic processes meticulously.

Bigging it up and dealing with the press is at its most important when your business is about to take a big step forward. Perhaps you are about to buy another business or perhaps you are about to take the idea that you grew from an acorn into an oak by expanding into a huge new market venture. Whichever it is, you are going to have to impress people with your professionalism and attention to detail.

Buying another business could mean running into the planning department of one or more local authorities. Here's an area where your professionalism is at a premium. Be careful; go through the bureaucratic processes meticulously. If you make one important mistake they will examine you very carefully and find out just out small and embryonic your business is. Take advice from people you trust. Planning departments have two things in common with elephants – they will move extremely slowly unless they see a jolly good reason to speed up and they never forget. Have a run in with someone in planning and they have your number and will treat you with suspicion the next time you need to get something through. They have been known to forgive and forget, but only after about 20 years.

Starting a new business is as exhilarating an activity as you can be involved in without taking physical risks with your body. (I imagine it's pretty exhilarating to take off from an aircraft carrier. But I've never tried.) Temper that exhilaration with logical thought and planning and you'll succeed. Your plan will never survive intact as the practicalities of real life test out your ability to react and solve problems as they arise. But the overall strategy of what you're selling to whom should survive the hazards of everyday business life.

One more thing – remember we talked about the owners of the business taking as little money as possible out of a new business? Here's where that comes in useful. If you've got cash you have a head start on those who don't.

We've got to take a break here from the heavy brainwork. What I am going to cover from here on in is how to make a business profitable fast and how to sell a business. For both of these tasks you need some financial knowledge – that's the bad news. The good news is that my next chapter on business finance will save you going to Harvard.

6

TEN KEY THINGS TO KNOW ABOUT BUSINESS FINANCE

Like it or not, finance is part of the language of business. Get to know enough about it to be able to talk to finance directors, bankers and so on without having one hand tied behind your back.

People come to the Den with the aim of securing investment and becoming entrepreneurs. They're there to get me to part with £50,000 of my money. But when I ask them straight questions about turnover or the state of their balance sheet they smile nervously and admit they don't know what that is. Which is why the money usually stays firmly in my pocket. Now, I'm not for a moment suggesting that you should become an accountant or even get close to having the knowledge and skills that an accountant has: that's what they're for and you can hire or rent them.

But if you've bought the right business or started a new one up, you're going to have to manage its growth. In the case of businesses that you have bought, in most cases you will need to turn it round from loss to profit; in order to do that you've got to have the basics of business finance in your head. It's like going to live in a foreign country. You don't need to be fluent in all aspects of the language but you just won't get on if you haven't got a firm grasp of the basics of everyday communication. In this chapter

I've summarized what I think are the top ten finance concepts that you need to understand, if not master. If you take them on board you will be in a good position to get on with managing your businesses. Perhaps more importantly than that, you'll be able to hold your own with a finance expert, confident enough to keep asking questions until you have understood what they are talking about. When you need to discuss financial detail with them, keep asking questions until the topic is clear in your mind. If you do this once it will stand you in good stead in the future.

What's in the finance top ten?

1 Look after the cash and the profits will look after themselves
2 Keep your cash flow document up to date
3 Charge the best price
4 Appreciate the impact of break-even analysis
5 Look for profits in after sales
6 Make money out of other people's money
7 Use the rule of 72 in compound interest
8 Choose whether to buy or rent
9 Understand the general business model and working capital
10 And so back to cash

1   Look after the cash and the profits will look after themselves
I once went into a conversation with two business people who were masters of their highly skilled trade but whose lack of business sense made me reel. They owed some £750,000 on an overdraft whose actual limit the bank had set at £700,000. They had their houses at risk as guarantees against the bank lending, and they were, to say the least, worried.

Looking around at the end of February I discovered that no one had sent out January's invoices. Not only that, but outstanding debts were well overdue. Their explanation was that they were too busy trying to deliver a service to a big customer in a contract that was worth a lot of money, and eventually a lot of cash. But that cannot be right. Make sure that invoices happen as soon as possible, that your collection terms are known by and agreed to by your clients, and put someone in charge of keeping the system up to date and chasing debt. Lots of companies simply do not pay their bills until someone chases for payment. Oh, and get payment up front whenever you can. You might even want to think of a sliding scale of invoices that rewards prompt payment and punishes the feet-draggers.

Tip from Shaf – Measure Your Cash Collection Success

Put in place a measure of how successful you and your people are in getting invoices paid. A simple way is to, on a monthly basis, add up your total invoices for the previous 12 months and divide it by 365 to give your average daily sales. Now take your debtors figure and divide it by that average daily sales figure to give your average collection period. If things are going well, or you deal a lot with cash customers, you may find your average collection period at about 30 days. If you are not putting enough effort into debt collection it could go up as high as 120 days. The point of doing this on a monthly basis is to monitor whether you are getting better or worse at getting your money in. If your collection period has gone up for three successive months: take immediate action, you have a problem.

You will have heard the expression KISS (Keep it Simple, Stupid) and it is without doubt good advice. In the end, trading is about two people representing two organizations offering a deal – 'If you do this, I will do that.' Try to keep your business focused on that simple concept.

TICK is the other key acronym for the person with his or her own business and it stands for Think in Cash, Knucklehead. Remember the mantra 'profit is opinion, cash is reality' and make sure that you have a firm grip on that reality. Companies do not actually go out of business because they run out of profits; Eurotunnel and many high technology businesses have not made a profit yet, but are still very much in business. No, companies go out of business because they run out of cash. So when you are starting, keep your projected cash flow up to date on at least a weekly basis.

What you are trying very hard to avoid with your bank manager is giving him or her a surprise of any sort. There are two reasons for this. Firstly, if you pitch up for the third time in a year cap in hand because you can't afford to pay this week's wages bill, the bank may very well call it a day. Their grounds for calling in the loans at that point could be that they simply do not believe that you have what it takes to control a business, and they want out while the assets can still be sold or your house still covers the outstanding borrowings.

In a start-up business or if you are in an industry such as building where late payments and going bust are endemic, your cash flow statement is probably the most important business process you have in place.

2   Keep your cash flow document up to date
Producing a good cash flow statement depends on four things, one of which should be easy, the second gets easier with time,

the third takes up much more time that you could possibly imagine and the fourth is a bastard.

1   An accurate estimate of your fixed costs. When you did your documentation for the bank you will have filled out the expenses and wages sheet that identifies your fixed costs. As you add to them, keep this number up to date. Remember this is a cash flow, so you do not include any depreciation that comes off your monthly profit and loss account. If you are depreciating fixed assets such as computer equipment, for example, the cash implication will be under capital expenditure on the week that you buy the equipment or in fixed costs as loan repayments if that is how you financed it. The value of the equipment, remember, is an opinion, we are only interested in the reality.

    Variable costs are those costs that only occur when you make products or deliver services.

2   Variable costs are those costs that only occur when you make products or deliver services. The cash flow will include the details of the money spent on production as it occurs. If you sell the services of consultants but they are on your books, then you should include them in fixed costs – you have to pay for them whether they are working or not. If you employ casual labour depending on having work for them, then you will have to become good at estimating your profit margin as you sell them on. So a building contractor will take a view on the percentage of sales that comes through as variable costs. It will not be very accurate but if you always reckon conservatively you should ensure a reasonably true picture. Think hard about your variable costs and improve your ability to estimate them and understand the timing of payments.

3   The third element of all this concerns your skills in getting your bills paid. Don't underestimate how much time needs to

be spent on it, and spend money on a resource to do it for you if it is taking up too much of your time.

4   And finally the bastard. The top line of a cash flow is dictated by the sales forecast, the most difficult estimate of them all. Not only do you have to guess how many units you will sell, you also have to estimate when the orders and deliveries will happen. Add to this the problem that you might not get all the orders you bid for because you will lose some to the competition. You know you will lose some, but which ones?

In the appendix on page 203 there is an example of a fairly rough and ready cash flow for a contractor with various levels of gross margin. An expert contractor prepared it, not an accountant. Finance professionals might find it a bit inelegant, but it does the job. Management can see what needs to be done to ensure a satisfactory cash position.

Review this on at least a monthly basis. Do it weekly if you are managing a difficult situation. The trick is to generate one that reflects your business very well, and needs little work to update it. Doing it without a spreadsheet on a computer is truly doing it the hard way.

3   Charge the best price

How much should you charge for your product or service? There is no fixed answer or formula to that question. The first key is to make sure you are charging enough to make a good profit. Don't forget that the profit you make on a deal has to make a contribution to all your fixed costs and overheads, as well as paying for the direct costs of the product. The second key is to make sure your pricing is competitive, but don't forget that reputation and trust have a value. If you give first-class, reliable service you might be able to charge a premium and risk not being the cheapest bid.

It's very important to charge the market price for your products. When you, like any salesperson, are selling to an important customer or a new customer it's the fear of losing to the competition that makes us go cheaper than we need. Customers and prospects will be looking at more than one option, and you have to think about handling price objections. Even if you're confident of your value to a customer and have tried to see it from their point of view, you will still be in competitive situations where the absolute price is a contentious issue.

Here are some simple techniques for dealing with a complaint about your price. In face-to-face and telephone selling we tend to react wrongly when someone comes up with the dreaded question, 'Sorry, mate, I've found a cheaper quote. What are you going to do about it?' What do you do when you hear these words? The best advice sounds rather counterintuitive – welcome price objections. After all if they are objecting to the price it sounds as though they think the product or service is right for them. And you will be more likely to manage the situation well if you appear confident. Breaking out in a cold sweat will harden the objection rather than loosen it. Price is getting more and more important in everybody's business. Intermediaries and consumers, using the Internet, can trawl for the cheapest price.

Consider the possible answers to the customer's question. You could try: 'We'll match it.' That may get the business but it also gives big problems with the profitability of the deal. You could try a re-iteration of the features and benefits of your proposal but that sounds heavy, is probably boring, and clients are unlikely to be swayed at this stage. In any case, they already think that an alternative offer is at least similar. Much better is to go back to the basis on which the customer is making their decision.

Try the return question: 'If we were the same price as the lower quote would you buy from us?'

What is the client to say? Suppose they say, 'Well, no actually.' This is the worst outcome, but at least you can now ask why, and deal with the other objections real or imagined. Suppose they say, 'Well, yes I think we would.' At that point the same question 'Why?' will elicit what the client believes are your advantages as opposed to your general claims. In this case clients are almost persuading themselves that the bit extra is worth it. Incidentally, the other selling technique that is tested by this method of handling price objections is the ability to remain silent and listen. Frequently the 'Would you buy from us if we were the same price as the cheapest?' question leads to a lot of thought from the prospect. Keep your mouth shut and wait for the response.

Everyone negotiates for everything, particularly in these hard times. This means that you will probably have to lower your price a bit during the negotiation; so, to begin with, ask for more than you would settle for. Remember you can always come down from your first price but the customer will never allow you to go up. In my experience of negotiating, setting the price for your first bid with as large a margin as you dare, generally gets a better result than going in only just above the price you are hoping for.

Always go into a negotiation with plenty of minor issues – terms of trade, delivery, payment times and so on. You might be able to make a concession on those that does not impact your profit nearly as much as reducing the price. For example, if you are dealing with a middle manager in a big company he may not be measured against an objective in the area of managing cash. This can give you the opportunity to improve the deal for you by offering a discount for prompt payment. That way you both win; they have done a better deal in cost terms and you have protected your cash flow.

I tried it and ...

> I have used this exact objection-handling technique twice recently, once successfully and once unsuccessfully.
>
> The first time I tried it I couldn't believe the length of the silence that followed my question. I had really made the customer think and I believe it showed that she was positive towards my offering. But I blew it. I couldn't stand the silence and asked another question. This got her completely off the hook and I lost.
>
> The second time I did it I held my nerve during the long silence and then the guy said, 'Well, I suppose I would actually.' He then reeled off why he preferred my proposal and I simply asked him if he thought that those extra benefits were worth the extra cost. He then asked for one very minor concession, which I gave him, and the deal was done. How come so many selling techniques are so simple and yet we don't use them?

4   Appreciate the impact of break-even analysis

As I've said, an alarming number of people go into business with little or no understanding of the financial side of running a business. I've spoken to one woman who is setting up a company. When I suggested she draw up a spreadsheet of her costs and estimated revenues she replied that she just couldn't get her head around figures and was going to leave all that to the accountant. To be honest, I think that's a bit like driving a car and only seeing road signs every 6 months. It's also like using the rear view mirror to plan the journey: you only know you've got a problem when it happened a while ago. I guess it's one of the reasons that I get so many opportunities to buy businesses cheaply and turn them round ...

I am quite happy for business people to be uncertain how accountants draw up the annual report from the bookkeeping figures, but I'm also convinced that you've got to understand enough about finance to help with two processes. Firstly, you need to know enough to use the numbers to help with planning, and secondly, you need to be able to read the signals that the numbers give on your progress. Of these signals, break-even analysis is by far the most important at the beginning of a new business project.

While you are still spending more money than you're receiving in sales revenues, you remain uncertain whether your dream business is going to come true or turn into a nightmare of sleepless nights.

The difference between success and failure in a new business revolves around how long it takes for the business to start making a profit. While you are still spending more money than you're receiving in sales revenues, you remain uncertain whether your dream business is going to come true or turn into a nightmare of sleepless nights.

Here's how it works. Every month you are going to spend money, whether anyone comes through the door to buy something or not. These expenses are called, quite reasonably, fixed costs. They include the rental or mortgage costs of the premises, insurances, staff costs, maintenance work, marketing costs and so on. As part of your plan you need to make an absolutely complete list of these. Don't miss anything out or the calculation will go horribly wrong.

I know two guys who bought a boat with the intention of offering a ferry service on a major river. It was a good idea. They were going to put a gym into it so that river commuters could do their exercises while they were on their way to work. But they didn't work out the numbers until after they had signed contracts for the boat. By the time they realized that the ferry service couldn't ever make a profit because of the way the costs worked out, they were down the price of the boat and up to their ears in debt. Good lesson there – make sure you have done an outline break-even analysis before you agree to buy any fixed asset or jump into any new product or service.

Other costs, apart from the fixed ones, are called variable costs. In retail premises, for example, these only really occur when a customer buys something. They are the direct costs of your product – the ingredients on the plate in the restaurant or the cost of the pen in the newsagent. The more you sell, the higher the variable costs, but thanks to their profit contribution, each sale helps counterbalance your fixed costs and subsequently improve your profits. People call it all sorts of things, like profit or margin, but I find the word contribution fits the bill best. When you have worked out the difference between what customers paid for your products and what you paid for them you have the *contribution* that the profit on that revenue has made to fixed costs.

Here's the formula in equation form:

revenues – variable costs = contribution – fixed costs = net profit

Make yourself a spreadsheet template of this formula and use it whenever you introduce something new into your business. It only takes a few minutes once you've got the hang of it and could save you, well, the cost of a redundant ferry.

What break-even analysis can do for us
Obviously you've got to know exactly what your fixed costs are and therefore your break-even point. Then you've got to know the variable cost of each item you sell. If you're selling gifts then

you will want to give a prominent display to items with a high mark up. But near the till you'll also want to display some cheap products with a small margin but the potential for a high level of sales. What you're hoping is that a fair percentage of customers add the cheap knick-knack to what they've already bought.

It's easy to remember to keep the fixed costs as low as possible, after all it's up to you how many staff you have on and what you pay them. It can be slightly more difficult to lean equally heavily on variable costs. There are, for example, salesmen for your suppliers trying to improve their margins. There's always the worry that if you find a cheaper source of ingredients or whatever, you may damage the quality of the product and lose customers and so on.

Keep people in your variable costs

As well as the profitability effect of having as few actual employers as possible there are some other benefits.

Firing poor performers is an expensive business, as is letting people go because you don't have the level of work for them that you were expecting. And don't underestimate the negative affect that this will have on morale. There is much less employee loyalty around now than was the case, mainly due to the behaviour of employers who, in reacting to very fast changes in the business environment, show markedly less loyalty in the other direction. This means that people are more than willing to move to a competitor.

So, if you make wrong decisions in staffing and have to put them right, you may find yourself with a morale problem leading to the loss of those people you desperately needed to keep.

One way out of this dilemma of 'Do we need another person and is this the right one', is to use temps and contractors. (Be very careful of the tax position on contractors, especially in the IT business. The Government is bearing down on contractors who use their employer's equipment and only have one customer. They regard such individuals of being in reality employees and want the tax and National Insurance contributions appropriate to that status.)

But temps and contractors are not in fixed costs. You can dispense with their services whenever you want and they are never regarded as full members of the team. This means that their departure is met with more equanimity than if they were. The two disadvantages of this approach are a higher daily rate cost and the fact that you have no hold over the people either. But remember, the more you have in variable costs, the more efficient use you make of fixed costs and the more you leverage up the profits.

5   Look for profits in after sales

Go out and buy a computer peripheral in a high street or mall shop. If you haven't done it for a while you will be amazed at how cheap things have become. You can buy a colour laser printer for just over £100. Think how much it would have been even two years ago. Now have a guess at what the retailer and the supplier are making in terms of contribution to their bottom line with that sale.

What happens next? You take it to the checkout counter and the salesperson asks you if you want extended warranty cover for a price that is not much less than 30% of the price of the printer. It's very good business for the retailer and gives you the reassurance that you will have the printer with no further expense for, say, 3 years. It's a win/win.

Now think about the price you will pay when the ink runs out; it could be again up to 30% of the price of the printer. It's still a win/win; you got the printer for a pretty good bargain price and the retailer and supplier got their profit from the after sales, the ink.

Tip from Shaf – If You've Covered Your Fixed Costs, the Rest is Profit

Many businesses cover their costs with their core business and make very profitable deals out of their add-ons. It's pretty true that a pub covers its costs with its drink and fattens the bottom line with its food, while a restaurant covers its costs with its food and makes its real profits out of the wine list. Make sure you are squeezing all the available profits out of potential add-ons to your business. Thinking outside the box is how entrepreneurs find new sources of income separate from their original idea.

Cheap package holidays are sold on extraordinarily tight profit margins, so they sell travel insurance amongst other services. Hotels regard the room price as just starters; using the rooms gets the guests into the bars and restaurants. More or less giving away compost-collecting bins to go in the kitchen allows all the big supermarkets to sell recyclable bin liners. Shoe shops sell expensive waterproofing cream to go with the shoes, hairdressers flog the same potions as they have just used for their client's hairdo and ... I think you've got the idea.

Thinking back to the break-even analysis tool, any manager or business owner needs that vital piece of information to enable them to find other activities whose gross profits go straight on to the bottom line.

There's a white goods shop not far from where I live that has a sign above its entrance saying, 'Through this door come the most important people in the world, our customers.'

Whenever a customer comes on to your premises, hits your website, is on the telephone to your company or contacting you in any other way, it is an opportunity to sell. Make sure you know what your related sales are and make the most of that important contact.

6   Make money out of other people's money
I am interested in both business finance and personal finance and making money out of other people's money spans both arts. Let's start with business finance.

Most successful entrepreneurs have at least a couple of things in common:

- They don't get so attached to a business that they cannot bring themselves to sell it. It's a good thing when an owner is passionate about their business, believing that they are providing an excellent product or service to their customers. If that is the case; they will put their heart and soul into making it work. They should, nevertheless, still be looking for the best time to sell it on, to realize the added value they have achieved in growing the profitability of the business. That's what an entrepreneur does.

- At some point in their careers entrepreneurs make use of other people's money to make money for themselves – this is called leverage.

Thinking back to the break-even analysis tool, any manager or business owner needs that vital piece of information to enable them to find other activities whose gross profits go straight on to the bottom line.

Here's how it works ...

Suppose a company has profits of £1 million. The owners are willing to sell it at a price/earnings ratio of ten. This values the company at £10 million. An entrepreneur buys the business using their own money of £1 million and borrowings of £9 million. The entrepreneur knows that through some synergies with other companies they can grow the business on a fast track in the short term. Suppose, then, that the business grows and within two years is running with profits of £2 million. On the same valuation, the business is now worth £20 million which, if realized, would pay back the debt and leave the entrepreneur with £11 million as return on the original stake of only £1 million – a rich return.

But remember this is all about risk; it works in reverse as well. If the business struggles and profits drop to £500,000, then the value of the business has gone down to £5 million and it still has debts of £9 million. In that case the original buyer would have lost their entire £1 million capital and have to find some way of paying off the debt or putting in even more money to get the company to trade its way out of the problem.

Another implication of debt is paying interest. Right now, with bank base rate at 0.5%, there is only one way that it can move – upwards. Take that into account when you are borrowing money to put into or buy businesses. Make sure that your calculations cover the fact that you may have to pay more for loans, particularly overdraft loans with variable rates. Suppose you are offered a loan at 3% above base rate to fund a deal. Just ask yourself if the deal would still make sense if base rates went up to say 4% over the next couple of years, making your loan interest 7%. Always look for the advantages of leverage but take the interest bill into account.

7   Use the rule of 72 in compound interest

This is a very useful rule of compound interest. Unfortunately it is not an exact formula so it does not work with very short timescales. But for timescales of longer than 2 years it works well enough. To calculate how long (in years) it will take for investment money to double at a given rate of compound interest,

Tip from Shaf – Buying Your Own House

Do the same rules of leverage cover a property you are buying using a mortgage? Well yes they do; but remember that the main purpose of buying your own home is to have somewhere to live. Right now, for example, banks are offering mortgages with the option of have the interest rate fixed for a period of time or taking their variable rate. At the moment [early 2010] they are offering around 4.7% fixed for 5 years or their current variable rate of 4.24%. This makes the variable rate a significant bit cheaper; but rates are going up. Using the laws of leverage, the lowest risk option is to go for the fixed rate for 5 years option. For most people this probably makes sense – don't make a big leveraged play on your own house – it's primarily a home not an investment.

simply divide 72 by the interest rate. Thus at an interest rate of 10%, money will double in just over 7 years. And you can use it the other way round. Here's an example. When I make an investment I want to at least double the money I am putting into a company in at the most 5 years.

If I want to double my money in 5 years what annual return will I require? 72 divided by 5 gives you a rate of roughly 14.5%. This gives me the minimum rate that someone pitching for me to invest must forecast the growth of their business's profits.

You will probably not use it so often, but as a matter of interest, so to speak, tripling your money works in the same way with the rule of 115.

In both cases treat the rules with care. As I said, it's not an exact formula and if it's important to work out an accurate number you'll have to use a spreadsheet.

8   Choose whether to buy or rent

Whether it's a family home or a full-on business, don't forget the value of the assets you or your businesses live in. You miss an opportunity if your landlord is the person making money out of the upward revaluation of properties. This gives me a bias towards buying property assets rather than renting – even including warehouse space.

Buying normally makes sense on the profit and loss account since the outlays to put capital in and borrow are less than the rents landlords charge. It stands to reason – they have to make a profit on top of the running costs of the property. If you buy, you get that profit and the capital appreciation. Another point, when a company goes into administration I buy the premises from the receiver: since, incidentally, banks don't have a clue about the proper valuation of properties there's opportunity there perhaps to buy at well below market value. In the property boom recently ended, a lot of businesspeople made more money out of the business premises they had bought than they made out of the businesses they were running inside them.

Generally speaking I can work out the financial results of doing a deal in my head. OK, it's not accurate to five decimal places but a quick piece of mental arithmetic normally tells me what I need to know. Buying properties can be an exception to that rule and I think it makes sense to get into the nitty-gritty of return on investment calculations if you have a complicated decision to make.

You will easily find people to argue the opposite of what I just said. So let's balance the 'always buy' view with a look at a different situation. A businessperson was trying to build a series of pubs and clubs in a town that had recently opened a second university. He much preferred to lease the premises because then he could use any extra cash that he had as a result of that decision to expand into the next premises and so on. To get rapid

Tip from Shaf – Calculating Return on Investment

Suppose you need a shop for the next stage of your business development. If you do want to make a decision based entirely on finance here's how to do it. Assume for the moment that all other things are equal; you will sell the same amount of goods from the shop however you occupy it, owner or tenant. Now make a 5-year cash flow of the out-goings involved for each method. Get the insurance side right and the rates and all the other expenses. Now discount the cash flow for time and arrive at the net present value of the two methods and decide on the better of the two. If you don't know how to do this, get your accountant to show you and don't leave his or her office until you can do it – it's the only sensible way to measure financial return on investment and an absolutely essential skill for someone building a business.

growth, he had to make the best use of his capital so leasing made sense to him. He leased the pubs, filled them with students and sold the chain as a popular and growing concern.

Consider the buy or rent decision carefully, but lean towards the buying side. Mind you, things can go wrong as well as right. Here's a situation that a pal of mine faced.

I tried it and ...

I bought a warehouse because it seemed to be the sensible thing to do. I then merged another company into mine and they had warehouse space as well. It made sense to combine the two warehouses into the new one. This left me with an empty warehouse at a time when it was very difficult to sell, given the way the market was going. So, I'm a bit lumbered.

This is a time for my friend to be ultra-realistic about the value of his asset. If he tries to rent it, he should set the rent as low as possible – even if it's just covering the costs of the warehouse. If he can't rent it he has no option but to think about selling it for a give-away price. I know it means he'll take a hit on his profits this year but the value of an asset is what someone is willing to pay for it. Meanwhile, the savings he's making from the combined use of the other property should help to get that money back and then some. It's a tough call but it's better for him to make it now than leave it, hope for the best and then find he needs to sell it for the same knock down price in two years' time.

9   Understand the general business model and working capital

How managers use cash

Once the owners and lenders to the business have put cash into the company's bank it is free to start trading. It will need to spend some of the money on fixed assets – buildings, vehicles and so on – but the main concern of middle managers is on working capital. This is the cash they are using to create products and services, sell them and provide after-sales support. Their main measures come down, in the end, to how quickly the cash flows round this working capital cycle.

The general business model

Now, I'm not a great one for the theories of running a business. I believe that we should keep everything as simple as possible. You've got to be able to look at a situation, break it down to its basics and see the profitable way ahead. Essentially running a business is about how cash flows round a business. Your task is to make that flow as efficient as possible. This general business model is a useful diagram of the process and may help you to drive business situations back to basics even when the situation seems rather complex. Here is the general business model:

The General Business Model

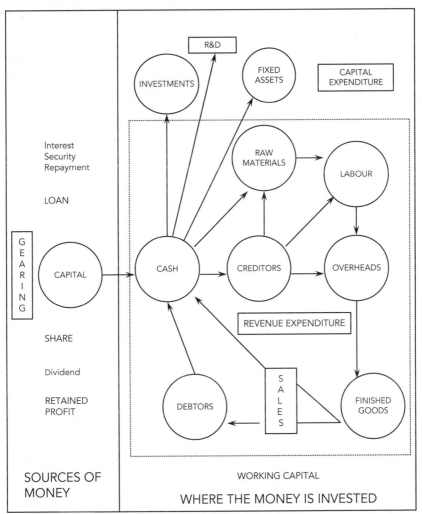

The capital employed in the business comes from shareholders and lenders. Share capital has the implication that the company will be expected to pay the forecast dividend. The undistributed part of a company's earnings stay in the business and belong to the shareholders. Retained profits, in most cases, increase shareholders' funds on an annual basis.

This capital goes into the company as cash, the first step in the working capital cycle. Managers spend this cash on, for example, raw materials, labour and overheads in the case of a manufacturer, or mainly on labour in a service business. Production, or the purchasing department, produces a stock of finished goods that are sold to customers for either cash or credit. In a service industry there is no stock, although there may be, in slow times, idle labour. Labour is not the same as stock, of course, because you can store stock for the future, idle time is labour lost. Also in the working capital cycle are creditors. These occur when materials or services that your company acquires from others are supplied on credit.

Here's an example of an industry that, because of the nature of their business, can excel in speeding cash round its working capital cycle.

In a service industry there is no stock, although there may be, in slow times, idle labour. Labour is not the same as stock, of course, because you can store stock for the future, idle time is labour lost.

From the recent accounts of a major food supermarket, we can see that it takes less than 20 days from when they receive goods inwards until the sales proceeds are in their bank account. Calculate their payment period to their creditors at 25 days and you find that their creditors fund all the supermarket's working capital needs.

It's not so easy when you are selling complex products to customers with time to study and compare before spending large sums of money.

A leading aerospace manufacturer in the same period, BAE, holds its inventory for over 100 days before it even starts to collect money from customers.

So from these physical examples we can see that ideally raw materials and parts will be incorporated into the product on the day they are delivered by the supplier. In this ideal world someone will buy each product as it comes off the assembly line into stock or inventory. And finally in this commercial Utopia, customers will pay their bills on the day that was agreed in the contract.

In fact, the world is not the ideal one described above and it takes considerable organizational effort to make businesses at least as efficient as their competitors or even with some sort of advantage to give them competitive edge.

There was a time when it was new thinking to plan to accept goods inwards 'just in time' (JIT). Manufacturers wanted their suppliers to deliver goods just before they were required. They were trying to create the ideal world described above. Many of their suppliers, particularly the smaller ones, found this very difficult. They found it difficult, given their chaotic business processes, to meet their customers' requirements. In fact, for some of them it was impossible to go round their order and delivery cycle inside the time their customers wanted delivery.

Trying to give this service, therefore, gave rise to makeshift ways of complying. It is said that a small supplier to a Japanese motor company in the UK kept a wagon-load of the parts they supplied in their customer's car park. When the call came through they instructed the driver to go from the car park to the goods inward area immediately – a good result for the car manufacturer, but an expensive solution for their supplier.

Expenditure on items within the working capital cycle is known as revenue expenditure, since its purpose is to create the revenue or income of the business. Revenue expense is an immediate cost which reduces the profits of the enterprise.

If a company generates profits it will normally also generate cash. Managers can use this cash for the long-term development of the business. Long-term investments are in fixed assets and research and development. A company can also invest cash in other companies, buying some or all of its shares as an investment. The full cost of capital expenditure is not normally taken off the profits of the year the investment is made but spread over time. This is known as depreciation.

Keep the general business model in your head as a simple template. There are some complications, but none that invalidate this picture.

10   And so back to cash

I was bound to do it – come back to cash. We've seen how having cash in the bank can make the difference between getting a deal now or losing it over time while you try to rustle up the money. Businesses, particularly small businesses, go bust not because they run out of profits necessarily but because they run out of cash. You can achieve a 20% return on capital employed, a pretty strong rate of profitability, and go bust at the same time.

Here is a simple example of a company whose profitability is unquestionable, but whose cash position does not just threaten its ability to pay dividends, but also its ability to survive.

Going bust profitably

Here is a company making a healthy profit. In fact, its return on capital employed is pretty good at 20%. There is nothing untoward either about its ability to pay its interest charges out of its profits. In fact, interest accounts for less than a third of its profits before interest and tax. Here are the numbers mocked up to make the point:

Long-term debt		**60.0**
Shareholders' funds		40.0
Capital employed		100.0
Return on capital employed	20%	
Profit before interest and tax		20.0
Interest rate	10%	
Interest		6.0
Profit before tax		14.0
Tax rate	25%	
Tax		3.5
Net profit after interest and tax		10.5

Unfortunately those numbers only show one of the implications of debt i.e. interest. Another one is making repayments. In this case the company has to pay back £12,000 a year on the five-year loan. Now look at the numbers:

Net profit after interest and tax (as before)	**10.5**
Repayments	12.0
Net cash outflow	-1.5

So, bad luck, they are making money and running out of cash. Keep a sharp eye on the cash and make sure there is a culture of being careful with cash throughout your organization and you'll probably survive.

7

MAKE A BUSINESS PROFITABLE FAST

I know, I know – nobody goes into business with the idea of making a loss, so every bit of business advice is about making a profit. As an entrepreneur, however, you have an extra factor – you're up against the clock. When I buy a business it's often because it is struggling and my job is to turn it around. What people forget, however, is that if you're in the business of buying, selling and moving on to the next deal then the time it takes to make that business attractive to others is key. Take five years to turn a business around and you might be a good (even great) businessman but you're not an entrepreneur in my books. Turn it around and sell it on in the time between breakfast and lunch however ...

A lot about selling a business is to do with the assets a business owns, and I will give you some examples of this later. I tend to be fairly focused on the property side of fixed assets, so that's where most of the examples will come from. There are, of course, many other types of fixed assets such as plant and machinery and technology, but for most businesses their main fixed assets are land and property.

Sell the business immediately!

Naturally you're expecting lots of advice on things to do to a company that will increase its value, and you'll get just that. Before we even get onto that subject, however, I have a thought for you; the fastest way of making a business profitable – do nothing to it at all. There are many things you can do to improve a business and make it more profitable but they all take time, and time, as they famously say, is money. So if there is a way make a company more profitable (for you at least) without changing a single thing about it, it's something you should definitely consider before buying an investment.

It may sound like magic to make a profit without doing anything but it's perfectly possible. The trick is simply to know the market better than the sellers and the other potential buyers and, of course, to be really close to the local business scene through your network of contacts and activities that keep these contacts up to date.

Sometimes you don't have to know how to turn a business around, you just have to know that there is a market for something that means you can buy it and sell it on for a profit. I once bought a property in Edinburgh at 9a.m. for £3.3m and sold it by 12 noon for £5.5m minus the £200,000 legal and professional costs. So that was a £2m profit before lunchtime. That's about the fastest way I know of making a business profitable. Now I know this is a dramatic example, but it can be done. It's all a question of appreciating the market value of a business or an asset.

The trick also is to be very clear in advance that:

- you are going in to a deal as an entrepreneur, not to run the company (see Chapter 1 – Are You an Entrepreneur?)
- you have a clear idea of the value of the business you are buying

- you have a buyer lined up who you are sure will pay more than you had to
- you have a plan B in case that buyer falls through – because the last thing you want is to see a deal based on lightning turnaround fall through.

This last point is extremely important because fast turnarounds are a risky business even by entrepreneur standards. If you are effectively trading something you don't want to end up owning you have to be 100% sure you are not going to end up holding the baby. Ideally you will have more than one buyer lined up for the resale and in a perfect world these should be ready to bid against each other. Be aware that in a quick sell-on scheme like this there are a number of things that can blow the whole thing out of the water.

Be very clear not to have confused your buyer's needs with their wants.

- Your buyer(s) getting wind of what you paid will seriously reduce your room for manoeuvre when it comes to negotiating, so that has to be kept very close to your chest.
- Speed is of the essence – you really don't want your buyers to know that the sale has gone through – they must be presented with a *fait accompli* along the lines of, 'I've got it, you want it; this is what it will cost you'.
- There's usually a reason why something is going cheap and the usual buyers haven't snapped it up themselves, so be very sure that you haven't overlooked a potentially deal-breaking problem with the opportunity.
- Be very clear not to have confused your buyer's needs with their wants (see Chapter 8 – Drive a Hard Bargain). If a conversation makes you think that business A would love to get its hands on the assets of business B but you could get in there

first and buy those assets then that's a great opportunity to do a deal. But if business A doesn't need those assets and it just likes the idea, then you'll find that when it comes to negotiating the second part of your deal you are talking to a buyer who doesn't *need* what you are selling and knows that you have no intention of holding onto it yourself.

- The way to avoid that is to ensure that either customer A really needs what you are going out to get, or that you have plenty of other options for disposing of it.

Options for disposing of things is pretty much what I do best, as you'll see later in this chapter.

Tip from Shaf – Buy from the Banks

Probably the fastest way to make money out of a business is to buy property that has been repossessed by a bank. When it comes to repossession, banks are primarily concerned with recovering the outstanding value of the debt, rather than the value of the property. What this means it that unless no payments were made since the original purchase, it is likely that some of that debt has been paid off – so the price a bank sets on a property is almost certainly less than its market value. Which means that even if property prices haven't risen since the property was first sold, you're still likely to make a profit by selling it on.

The quick fix

Just because you can't sell something on immediately doesn't mean that it's yours for life. It's not just a case of sell it now or get used to it, because with a lot of companies the best deal may be to fix a problem you've identified, and then offer it back to the market. This may sound a bit crazy but in some cases the first step to fixing something may be for you to buy it. In some cases the fact that you were interested in something may mean others were too but they were just a little less daring. My own way of doing business is usually based on taking the plunge where others are still dipping their toes. In some markets, such as property, it can be the case that a number of potential investors are eyeing an area or a building and the moment the first one moves it confirms the idea that it was a good opportunity. It's at this point that everyone else wants part of the market and the price goes up. I'll give you a practical example.

Some time back I had the idea to create a block of very high specification flats. That idea came from an examination of a number of factors.

- There are a number of quality ex-industrial buildings that have fallen into disuse in an up-and-coming area.
- There is a growing class of highly qualified professionals in Edinburgh.
- I personally have a background in technology and understand that to really satisfy modern demand, the next generation of upscale professionals want networked home entertainment with home cinema, wi-fi, and integrated games and you need to build that from scratch, you can't just run an extension cable.

It was a great idea. No, scratch that, it still is a great idea but it requires investment not just in building purchase but also renovation costs, technological investment and market research. I took the first step and bought the old Martin & Frost building in Leith for £3.3 million. It was a former warehouse and I planned

80 two-bed top-flight flats. Then of course the affects of the credit crunch became known and I started to think that perhaps even the high-flying yuppies were going to struggle to get the borrowing needed from the banks. I still like my original plan but the timing turned against me.

So did that leave me holding the baby? Well not really, because the first of those three factors above was just sound business sense anyway and I had bought into a good building in a good location. The thing to do now was to find someone who simply had to have accommodation with or without a credit crunch. The fact that I had bought the property meant that a number of other buyers were now looking at it wondering whether they should have moved first. Of course it helps if you have a reputation as a canny operator, but even without that prices are often kick-started by the first-mover buying into a new opportunity. So I was able to sell the property for a handsome profit – it's going to become student accommodation. Of course what that says to me is that there is another generation of high-earning professionals on its way and so I'm keeping my eyes on that one.

Can you fix it?

There are a number of types of 'quick' fixes (quick in this case is defined by how much you can afford to wait and plough money into something), depending on the type of business and the nature of its problems. Amongst the areas you'll want to look at are:

1   cutting costs
2   spreading costs
3   sales and marketing
4   diversifying.

1   Cutting costs

There are often plenty of cost-cutting exercises that are easier for a new broom to do than for the old owners with their well-established ways. Changing suppliers is often a good start, since loyalty rarely breeds best pricing. Outsourcing is another very fast fix in a lot of cases. Companies are often so used to the idea of working in one particular way that they no longer analyse what it is they are really best at. So you get companies with a great line in new product ideas being hamstrung by old manufacturing processes and production lines and high wage costs, when really they could do themselves a huge favour by outsourcing manufacture entirely. That cuts cost and just as importantly gives them the agility to switch product lines quickly, meaning they can now diversify (more about this later).

There's another reason for outsourcing where possible; by stripping the business down to its core, that is the part of the business you cannot outsource, so it often becomes easier to see why the company isn't making the money it should.

Essentially most companies, whether they are providing products or services, work on the basis that pricing is set by the simple formula of cost plus margin. Which is great and tried and trusted and that's why nothing can go wrong with it.

The problem is that time and time again people overlook parts of their costs; perhaps because they're not aware of them, perhaps because they're allowing emotions to dim their vision when it comes to a particular part of the business, but it only takes one extra factor on the cost side to throw the whole cost-plus-margin calculation out of kilter.

You probably think of costs in terms of the following:

- materials
- stock
- labour
- marketing
- general overheads
- storage, handling and packaging
- transport and distribution
- depreciation of assets
- utilities

and if you're on the ball you also remembered to take into account these:

- rent
- council tax
- renovations.

But did you remember to include insurance and interest charges? Did you check the mark up of the distributor and see what your margin is compared to the final cost to the consumer? Did you allow for seasonal variation and the affect that has on for example warehousing – my favourite oft-forgotten factor? Margin means nothing if you haven't also taken into account the number of sales. Fixed costs remain just that, fixed, but if sales fluctuate then the money available to cover them will vary hugely. Failing to account for market fluctuation is a common cause of failure amongst businesses that otherwise look just fine.

If margins are tight, then you're going to have to cut costs and that means examining every angle of the expenses – preferably before you make that deal and buy the company.

These days there are excellent websites comparing the offers from different utility suppliers, and there are online bidding sites where you can put an offer to tender and see what new suppliers can do to undercut your current costs. I'm a *Failing to account* great believer in using the web to find the best *for market* deals going. Even if you don't really want to *fluctuation is a* take a chance on totally new suppliers there's *common cause of* nothing quite like putting everything out to *failure amongst* tender to put a fire underneath current suppli- *businesses that* ers. You might think you can't get bids for rent *otherwise look just* and tax but you can if you're prepared to relo- *fine.* cate or outsource. Think carefully about what you can cut and don't take anything for granted – it could just be the case that you can take the whole company online, make it virtual, and in the process of removing any premises totally reorganize its fixed costs.

If all of that sounds sweeping it's because I believe that cost cutting is not about penny pinching but rather about big shifts in attitude and thinking. Done right there doesn't need to be anything petty about cost cutting at all. What I hate doing is the kind of cost cutting that means going through the stationery cabinets and deciding on a cheaper brand of pencil. My head, however, knows that if you can't make big cuts elsewhere then the chances are it's not the stationery cabinet that's the problem. If you waste too much time on the small stuff you just won't have time to grow big. Don't look at cost cutting as a necessary evil – instead try to see it as a business opportunity and another chance to challenge your imagination and demonstrate your flair.

Another big area to look at when trying to make a business profitable in a hurry is to restructure its debts or accelerate its cash flow. Too many times you see companies that aim to make sweeping cuts, say 10% across off all fixed and variable costs, but who don't dare grasp the nettle of debt and cash flow. Nobody likes looking at debt, but if you're an entrepreneur and you have bought a company with debt you'd better know its extent and terms right down to the last penny. If you've bought a company out of bankruptcy then you're usually not liable for its debts but if you've bought a going (but struggling) concern then debt and cash flow should be the first things you look at. Typically, small businesses don't go about managing debt in a very joined up way. It starts with personal overdrafts and loans secured on property then creeps into unsecured loans and even heavy credit card borrowing (to be avoided at all costs) as the company struggles to keep cash flowing.

So start off by drawing up a full audit of all loans and of all debtor money owed to you. Bearing in mind what you're paying to borrow money, you should start by slashing the time that customers take to pay you. Consider using third parties to recover money if it really looks like the time and effort involved is going to be huge. Remember that if you're borrowing on the one hand then slow payment from customers can wipe out the profit on the deal, so speed it up.

Then take a look at the company's existing loans and see if you can replace that debt with a loan at a lower interest rate. Replace unsecured lending with secured loans; that will help to bring the rate down and see if you can't get guaranteed loans from shareholders to replace more onerous debt. Be careful, though, not to trade off too much control in return for that.

Sort out debt and cash flow and it's quite possible that your purchase is now ready for resale at a modest profit simply because there are a lot of risk-averse investors out there. They won't get their hands dirty shaking out a debt-ridden business, but they will probably be glad to take it off your hands once you've shown that it is not a basket case.

Tip from Shaf – Understand the Repercussions of Asset Stripping

If you're cynical about cost cutting then the fastest way of making money out of a business is often to wait until it fails then cut the cost of the business to zero by pulling the plug and selling the assets. This chapter, however, isn't about asset-stripping, so all I'll say about it is that if that's your game then make sure you understand the difference between buying a business before and after it goes into receivership (with the former you also inherit the liabilities) and do take into account all the other factors involved in such a deal, such as the reputation asset stripping creates for the stripper, the way that reputation may affect other deals, and the impact it will have on the people involved with the stripped business.

I'm not against asset stripping *per se*, it may be the only logical thing to do but if you look at the way I work both in the Den and with companies like Tiger Advisors and www.boffer.co.uk, you'll see that I prefer the challenge of mentoring and working with people and businesses to get them up and thriving. Of course that's easy for me to say; I've made my money and I'm now as interested in the challenge of a deal as the cash involved. Even so, you might want to think twice before taking an approach that will change the way you are seen by others. Don't forget that there is often more than one way to skin a deal. I've had some success before now where I've had my eye on the buildings of a failing company, but I've done a deal that lets them wind up the business and move on within a certain time so we both get something out of it.

FAQ – How Quick is a Quick Turnaround?

Q: *I've got my eye on a business that's struggling and I can see a number of options to turn it around, including outsourcing and licensing, but I'm worried about your insistence on speed. What sort of time frame should I be looking at?*

A: It's a bit of a 'how long is a piece of string question', but the thing to remember is that unless you're a very lucky person, your resources aren't infinite; time and money are closely related, as you'll know if you've ever worked out what compound interest is. You have to look at how long you can fund a company before it reaches profitability and what that funding will cost you over time. If you have your own money that's fine, less of a rush, but if you're borrowing then the cost rises every day to the point where it won't be worth it. The other key factor is that you always want to sell from a position of strength. If you start a turnaround and the business looks set to prosper but not for a while yet you can always try to sell it on then and there at a mark up. If you hold on too long and run out of cash, on the other hand, then you'll be forced to sell for whatever you can get. Hence, I'd go for a faster sale at an acceptable price rather than holding out for a promise of more jam tomorrow. Don't forget I make a lot of money out of buying businesses that other developers took on, waited too long for, and ended up selling for break even or possibly a loss. Don't be one of those.

2   Spreading the cost

Now this, on the other hand, is a brilliant way of making not just one but often two businesses more profitable at a stroke. This is part of the idea of synergy discussed elsewhere in the book and the point is to look for opportunities where one of your assets can work better by combining with another. A truly great partnership quickly becomes more than the sum of its parts because both companies are free to grow faster and deliver higher profits. My own experience with E-Net Distribution saw me create one of the world's largest distributors of optical storage products and that taught me a great deal about maximizing return from distribution channels. Perhaps it means I'm biased and tend to look at that angle first, but when I see companies in trouble I can so often pin the problem down to logistics, warehousing or wholesalers and that's usually the point where I think to myself – 'I could do something with this'.

So much so, in fact, that one of my investments is in a company that shifts unsold goods for retailers struggling with the crunch. Lots of companies have run into the problem that they're left with too much stock on their hands, but if they let that be known then prices will tumble further and they'll end up with nothing more than a fire sale. But I happen to have extensive warehousing and distribution networks in place from my other businesses. So what I'm doing is putting those two things together in a perfect example of synergy.

I've bought a 70% stake in CPM Asset Management, which was set up by a pal of mine going back 15 years (another reason to keep in touch with talent as discussed in Chapter 4 – Invest in People, Not in Products). CPM buys unwanted stock and sells it on to other businesses for a profit – on the condition that the retailer remains unnamed. A lot of retailers don't want to admit they have cash flow issues so something like CPM offers a discrete way to dispose of stock while ensuring it doesn't actually go to a competitor. Then we agreed to supply a number of websites, including www.boffers.co.uk and Estock (www.Estock.co.uk), who all started specializing in selling excess inventory to consumers and businesses. Now we have a whole marketplace based around stock that previously couldn't be offloaded, just by joining up the dots in distribution. Finally, I have a stake in the discount shopping website www.boffer.co.uk which sells one product per day. It also has an auction section called BOTS (short for 'Bit On The Side'). To our surprise, it was the BOTS section which showed the potential to become the most profitable part of the business. As I write, the programmers are rewriting the website to expand this section. The *boffer* BOTS cuts the price of goods every day until supplies run out. The idea is that a TV, for example, will go on sale for £1,000 on *boffer* BOTS. If no one buys it within three minutes the price will drop to £950 and continue to fall until it goes. What that means is that we have multiple points of sale along the chain. We haven't had to manufacture anything, we're doing everyone a favour, and profits look good. This brings us nicely to one of the most obvious, but most commonly overlooked, aspects of any business – increasing sales.

3   Increase your sales and marketing

When businesses get in trouble they often take it for granted that the way out isn't to sell more – they think that's the problem that put them into this position. So instead they turn to cuts. That's not such a bad thing in itself, as explained earlier, but it must be done intelligently. The outstanding knee-jerk reaction to improving profitability I often see is that the first thing to be cut is the emphasis on selling more. So, the first thing you see slashed is the advertising and marketing budget. This tends to be a short-sighted view and perhaps the opposite of the most successful strategy. It's time to think outside the box again.

There are many ways of increasing sales. The example of what I'm doing with CPM is a good one – I'm offering thousands of sales to companies that were previously staring at stock they couldn't offload. Obviously I'm doing it at a price that suits me but the cash flow implications for some of those companies will probably make the difference between survival or extinction for them. So think about different ways of selling what you've got before you start thinking about firing all the staff and selling the building.

The marketing budget is often the first to go precisely because it seems so expendable. There's always been the old joke about half the marketing budget being a complete waste, but nobody is sure which half. Truth be told a lot of companies are a bit mistrustful of marketing and the people who work for it, so when times are tough it seems normal to turn them outdoors first.

Truth be told a lot of companies are a bit mistrustful of marketing and the people who work for it, so when times are tough it seems normal to turn them outdoors first.

Normal, maybe, but that doesn't always make it the right thing to do. Selling your way out of a tight spot is always a great strategy, but unless you have found a new route to market (like the CPM example) you've still got to tell people what it is you've got and why they need it. For me one of the most wonderful things about the web is that it's such a fast way to reach people at a relatively low cost. So if you're looking at a company that's tight on cash but needing to get the word out then why not look at online marketing strategies – depending what it is you're looking to sell, the answer could be just to open a different line of communication to the customer and these days that could mean SMS marketing by mobile phone, a location-specific application for an iPhone ('you're passing by my restaurant – pop in now for 10% off'), or a Facebook campaign. Too many good companies have sunk without a trace because they simply didn't get the word out that they had something worth buying.

4   Diversifying

I touched on this when I mentioned outsourcing. The thing is that too many businesses get stuck in a rut. They use the same old suppliers, the same old manufacturing techniques, the same route to market, and it becomes accepted as if it was some kind of law just because it's always been done that way; then the market changes. A new product hits the market or someone else changes their pricing strategy or things simply go out of fashion and suddenly the business is on its knees because it didn't adapt. Some one-trick ponies do very well from sticking to their core business and there's a lot to be said for knowing what it is you do well and focusing on that. I believe, however, that if you take the time to analyse what it is you do well you could find that it could be applied to something else, even something very different indeed. Apple could have stuck to making successful computers but they moved into music players. This had the effect of turning the mobile phone market on its head. Now Nokia, the giant in that area, is left playing catch up.

So think carefully about what it is the business does best and try asking these questions.

- Should you sell a service?

If the business is making a product and doing well, then is there any market for selling that skill in the form of consultancy for example?

- Should you sell a product?

The reverse is also true – selling services is time and labour intensive but if there's any way of turning your service into a product it could transform your business. Training services, for example, can easily be supplemented by DVDs to be sold alongside the courses.

- Should you sell someone else's product/service?

Perhaps extending the range of what you do with complementary products could make your offer that much more compelling. Time to swallow the pride and look around at what other people are doing that could help put the sparkle back on your own business.

I tried it and ...

"Economies of scale often mean that smaller businesses fail where bigger ones survive and I've made some nice deals by finding small print companies that are going into receivership and buying them up. Then, by a mix of diversification (into packaging for example in one case) and sharing material costs to bring costs down, I've made them a better business together than they were apart. Working as one business, they were able to pitch for bigger, more lucrative jobs. The irony is that some of the businesses I buy and pair up were originally rivals and often went down together rather than team up under their original owners."

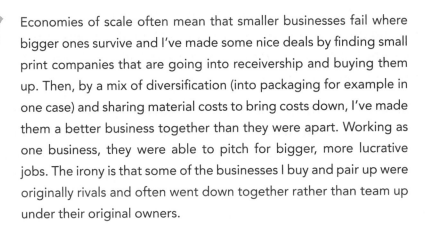

Tip from Shaf – SWOT

It sounds like something that abseils down from the ceiling, and properly used it can be just as effective. The SWOT (strengths, weaknesses, opportunities, threats) analysis technique can help you get to the point of just what it is that a business does well and from there you're in a better position to decide if outsourcing, cost sharing or diversification are the best choices open to you for turning a business around.

Pull together a team of key people in the new business and have each one identify the SWOT for the business from their perspective. Then get them all to propose answers to the following:

- how can we capitalize on our strengths?

- how do we improve on the weaknesses?

- how do we exploit those opportunities?

- what can we do to cancel out those threats?

Turning a business round is, as usual, more a matter of common sense than genius. Follow the pattern I suggest and you should find the strategy for making a business with potential into a business making money. This is particularly true if you have bought the right business and realized some synergies with other businesses in your portfolio.

Whatever the strategy, it is going to involve persuading other people to do things differently. It will also involve driving better deals with staff, suppliers or customers, or a combination of all three. For this, you need skills in negotiation, which is the topic of the next chapter.

8

DRIVE A HARD BARGAIN

There's a lot of rubbish talked about negotiation. To hear some people describe it you would think it was as complex and sophisticated as a game of chess – all about moves, counter-moves and strategy. Listen to others talking about their tips for negotiating and you would think they were describing some kind of blood sport – all about intimidation and strong-arming your way to getting what you want. In my experience it's neither of those. The secret to negotiation is so simple that it annoys me to see that so many people still get it wrong. Do your homework, know what you want, and always be ready to walk away if it doesn't look like you're going to get it. That's it. You can put the book down now and go out and make a million. Only you won't, because the chances are that like so many other people you don't believe it can be that simple.

People tell me I can be scary on *Dragons' Den Online*. There's talk about me 'savaging' candidates as if I leap out of my chair – all jaws and claws – and tear them limb from limb. Watch the programmes again on YouTube and you'll notice that I never get angry, loud or aggressive. What I do sometimes though is sit there open-mouthed at how badly prepared someone is. When that happens, I usually run through the most basic questions with them again to ram home the fact that they haven't got a clue and then I give up. So what are the basic questions you need to know the answers to?

What homework is there to do?

When I sag back in my chair with my mouth open I'm not angry – I'm shocked, dumbfounded that people go into a bargaining position with their dreams and future at stake and don't seem to do the most basic homework before they get there. Perhaps they don't know what needs to be done. Time and time again I ask the same questions:

- Have you done any market research?
- What are your profits?
- What are your projections?
- What are they based on?

It's not rocket science but you'd be amazed at how many people come onto the show and don't have the answers to those questions. Time and time again I ask someone what their profit is and they start to tell me about their turnover. I ask to see a balance sheet and they aren't sure what that is. I ask what the profit margin per unit is and they start to bluster about how they're sure that they can outsource to the Far East. I don't want to know about the ifs and maybes – I just want a straight answer to a straight question. If a businessman can't give me that about their business then I either think they don't know what they're doing or they're not being strictly honest with me. And this is when they are hoping to start a negotiation for money for shares in their business ...

I'll give you an example. We once had a chap in the Den who wanted me to back his business selling a kind of card game. To date, he'd been giving the games away free on the Internet but now he wanted to charge a quid for each one. His projection was that he would sell a million of them in the first year of charging. I asked how many he'd given away during the year they'd been free and the answer was 80,000. Now it's not impossible to shift from giving something away for free to asking for payment, a lot of computer games give away tasters online and then ask for payment for example, but they have a clear strategy – usually the payment unlocks the full game. In this case I asked why the demand for the games would increase more now that they would cost a pound, rather than when they were free. This chap had no answer to that. I'm sorry but if you haven't thought that far down the line then what are you doing trying to negotiate a deal with a backer?

There are many factors that can influence the way a negotiation goes but generally the rule is that the person with the most information is likely to do best.

That information can take different forms depending on the type of business, but there are certain basics that you absolutely need to nail down before you even think of walking into a negotiation to buy or sell a business.

Costs, profits and projections

This means having a solid grasp of all the costs of a business, of the income, the turnover, the cash flow, the gross profit and the net profit. Look back through Chapter 3 for guidance on how to turn that information into an estimated value of your and other businesses. It does mean that you need a clear understanding of the factors that are likely to affect future growth, including markets, demand, materials' costs, licensing and outsourcing possibilities.

What it doesn't mean is being lazy and plucking figures from the air. It doesn't mean deluding yourself with ludicrous figures based on nothing but wishful thinking either; but I've lost count of the number of times I find someone, inside and outside the Den, trying to bargain on the basis of wishful thinking instead of hard facts.

Industry knowledge

Depending on the business and the kind of role you intend to play, preparation is also likely to include a detailed understanding of the industry in question – the trends, the players, the long-term and short-term prospects. You don't necessarily have to drown yourself or your potential investor in technical detail, however. In fact, avoid giving too much information to an investor; you can't bore your way to concluding a successful negotiation.

> *Depending on the business and the kind of role you intend to play, preparation also is likely to include a detailed understanding of the industry in question – the trends, the players, the long-term and short-term prospects.*

I run E-net Distribution, one of Europe's biggest importers and distributors of optical media (CDs, DVDs, etc.). It also deals in digital storage products such as USB memory sticks and MP3 players.

I don't know need to know what the insides of a USB memory stick look like or how they work in order to come up with a business plan. What I need to know is the hard facts like the stark realities of cost per unit and the challenges of selling more product into an increasingly saturated market. Things like that make business tougher, but shy away from the challenging issues and you will gradually lose sight of your business's real value. What I see over and over, both in the Den and outside, are people who have either never come to grips with the hard facts, or prefer to look away from the ones that indicate a problem that needs dealing with. At this point I often understand the realities of their market better than they do. Make sure you're the person with the most knowledge and information if you want to get what you're after in a tough negotiation.

Set your limits

The first limit I tend to set is the point at which I will walk away. It's worth having a look in an auction room to talk to people who have either not done this or, more likely, in the excitement of the auction, go above the limit on what they would pay.

Be prepared to walk away by setting a limit on what you will pay for a business or a product or service – and stick to it.

At the other end of the spectrum, I set what I would regard as my best result. What would I be delighted to achieve? That then becomes my objective, but I do know that unless I have misjudged the situation of the person I am dealing with I will probably have to make some concessions. I know in advance what these concessions are and if the other party tries to make me concede more then I will ask for an adjournment rather than give way there and then. All I am saying here is that your preparation must include making a plan.

Here's a summary of what you need to make that plan.

- Set negotiations on your terms – don't be pushed into something. Decide on a time and place for the negotiation and then draw up a list of the following:

- What do I want? Think carefully about this. Are you really after profit, pride of ownership or just a piece of the action?
- What's the least I will settle for and be content?
- What's the best result I can imagine?
- What am I prepared to pay/sacrifice to get the least I will settle for?
- What am I prepared to pay/sacrifice to get the best-case scenario?
- What am I ready to compromise on?
- What are the unmoveable deal breakers from my point of view?
- Only if you are clear on all the above are you likely to get a positive result.

Do you know what you want?

You might think you know what you want – riches, success, a shiny Aston Martin in the garage and the respect of your mates, but that's not enough to graduate from the dreamers' club and cut it as an entrepreneur. Instead, you need to focus on each individual step and that means examining every situation to decide exactly what you intend to get out of it. Too many times people go into discussions, meetings and especially arguments without a clear idea of what they want to come out with when the dust has settled.

People who come to the Den don't usually know how much of their business they're prepared to sell. It's all just a made up figure for them because they haven't done the figures and worked out what they are likely to get from the deal. We once had a singer/songwriter who was effectively offering a cut of himself. I didn't go for it but fellow Dragon Julie Mayer immediately went for 51% of the deal. The singer seemed puzzled by the figure, seemingly unaware that it meant she was bidding for the minimum involvement that still gave her an unquestionable controlling share. Often people just react to figures with gut reaction. If I offer to take a 90% share in most people's companies they baulk and say no because it sounds like I'm taking over. But they need to think carefully about whether their goal is to own the controlling stake in that business, or whether they'd like a guaranteed 10% share of something that is going to make millions.

Given that most of the people who come to us in the Den are going nowhere fast as sole owners of their business, you would think that they would have the sense to know that 10% of even £1,000,000 is a lot more attractive than 100% of an outstanding bank loan. They haven't crossed the bridge yet between deciding whether they're trying to be an inventor, the owner of a business or an entrepreneur. That's a decision you want to make before you find yourself standing in front of any investor. In simple terms, I know exactly what I want out of negotiations in the Den. I want a share in what I think will be a winning business and a percentage of that business which reflects the amount of time and the skills that I or my people will put into the business to make sure it happens.

Do you know what you need?

Being aware of what it is you *need*, and what it is you *want* is one of the keys to personal happiness. It's also the secret of a good business negotiator, with a twist: that the really great negotiator goes one step further and also considers what the other person thinks they *want*, and what it is they really *need*. Separating out the 'needs' from the 'wants' sounds like a simple point, but it's actually one of the toughest questions you'll ever ask yourself –

really it means not only taking a realistic look at your life, but also at defining who you are, and what you expect to become. No wonder then that most people shy away from it altogether.

The problem is that so many people, asked to think about what they need rather than what they want, struggle to differentiate between the two. Instead they kid themselves by thinking not about what they want, but instead about what would be 'nice to have'. Then they mentally classify those 'nice to have' elements as things they might sacrifice at a pinch and tell themselves they've distinguished between needing and wanting. So, for example, they think that it would be nice to have a new BMW saloon, but they're prepared to put up with the ageing Toyota that's in the garage. Actually, they never had the BMW, or the money for it, so they've just 'compromised' by scaling down a pipedream. In reality, the truth might be that what they need is to give up running a car altogether and sell it to further fund the business.

It's not a compromise to sacrifice something you don't and may never have. Similarly, in business negotiation it gets you nowhere to 'compromise' by accepting that you might sell your business for £5 million instead of £10 million if in reality you have no precise valuation of it, or an understanding of just how much money you need to move on. If you don't know these things, these needs, you are vulnerable in negotiation to someone who steps in and tells you precisely what it is worth and why you don't need anything like as much money as you dreamed. Most people only learn what they really need (rather than want) when their backs are up against the wall. The trick is to work it out long before you get there.

If you know that all you need to make it to the next step in your business is to sell your current assets and make a 10% profit then you're well placed to negotiate. If, instead, you just have an idea that you want to sell this business and be rich, well, then you are not so likely to drive the bargain and may end up holding out while potential buyers walk away.

What you *want* is usually a list as long as your arm. What you *need* often comes down to some very simple bare necessities.

Start with what you need. If you have dependants, then you'll have to start with those needs: anything that threatens your ability to feed, house and generally care for them goes into the 'need' column. This might be quite a low threat if your partner is in a position to be earning enough to meet those needs. That's the easy bit.

Likewise, issues like a salary for yourself that covers those needs can be quite easily calculated and most entrepreneurs are happy to forego all but the necessities when they start out. Of course there is a lot of 'wiggle room' when it comes to 'necessities'.

For some people, enough money to buy food and a bicycle to get to work is the bottom line. For others a smart car and a designer suit are essential to maintain status with investors and co-workers. That's a call you're going to have to make for yourself, but break down all your likely expenses and be brutal about whether they are contributing to your business or just your ego. I know that sounds a bit rich coming from a man who used to change his Aston Martin several times a year, but the Aston is pretty much my only obvious vice. I don't live in a mansion or blow it all on bling. For some time I used to tell the neighbours that the car belonged to my boss, as that was easier than explaining what it was doing outside a fairly modest house in a fairly modest neighbourhood.

Once you've sorted out your material needs and factored them into producing the price tag of any deal, it's time to turn to the really tough question – what exactly do you *need* from this deal, as opposed to just what you want?

If you're on the selling side you need to think about your game plan. If you are deep in the hole of debt with people counting on you, then your need is the sum that digs you out. If the size of debt or the absence of debt means that you've got room for manoeuvre, you have to think about whether this deal is your one shot at your goal or if it is a strategic stepping stone – just a card to play to get you into the next level of the game. If you're emotionally attached to the company/property/deal then it's time to start thinking some of those unthinkables – like a project ceasing to be your baby if that's what it takes to move on and get what you really need.

If you're on the buying side of the deal, then your needs tend to be much more clear cut. Consider what kind of percentage markup you intend to make and think about what period you expect to make that in. Quite simply if a deal isn't likely to reach your target profit within a target period then you have to believe that there is always another deal to be done somewhere else. You'd be surprised how many people forget that and don't walk away.

Don't forget that a deal is rarely as simple as an object and a price. There are often a number of different ways of trimming and shaping it so that it can be made more attractive to either or both parties. The time line of any deal is often an issue – are either of you in a hurry? In this case a smaller sum in the short term may have more value than a slightly larger one over a longer period.

Can the deal be divided up into a number of different assets? I've certainly seen cases where I've offered to buy a failing business because I liked the look of the property it's housed in. In this case I look to cut deals that allow the owners ways to wind up their existing business and take out some profit from that, rather than just arguing over a lump sum here and now. The trick to breaking a deal down into its components is to take a long hard look at it yourself, but then to ask your opposite number what they value and want from it all.

It could be that the factor holding up the deal or artificially inflating the price is as simple as saving face. It's not uncommon for someone to hold out just because they feel that accepting your (lower) offer makes it seem that they are weak in their own eyes or those of their peers and partners.

I've certainly seen cases where I've offered to buy a failing business because I liked the look of the property it's housed in.

So see if you can add a new angle to the deal, one that doesn't just involve the price tag. Perhaps that person just wants a role of some kind with you. Perhaps they're trying to protect the job of someone else. You'd be surprised what comes up when people get really honest about deals. I know a man who wanted to sell his Mercedes but couldn't shift below a certain price – he'd paid a lot for it and it had become a sore point with his girlfriend about why the money hadn't gone into their catering business. In the end he found another catering business going into receivership and agreed a trade of the car for some professional coffee machines. The swap took away the emotional issue of the exact sum involved and everyone was happy.

Working out what you want and need and, perhaps more importantly, doing that for the other side is a good test of your ability to think laterally or outside the box. It is a great negotiating tactic to throw in a new consideration that meets the other side's needs or wants that they had never thought of.

Before you go into any negotiation you must have a clear idea of what it is you need, must have, or want, how you identify your desired result, what your best case is, what you would settle for if it came to that and, above all, what you are prepared to pay for all those eventualities.

Are you always ready to walk away?

This is the absolute make or break law of negotiation. OK, perhaps there are some negotiations where so much is at stake that nobody should ever leave the table – peace treaties, for example. But we're talking about business here and the best way of keeping your advantage in any negotiation is to have one eye on the door and to know exactly when it's time to turn on your heel and walk out.

These are tough times and they have driven people to do deals they wouldn't have looked at twice in better days. For a lot of businesses the need to maintain cash flow is more important than pretty much everything, including profit margins, in the struggle to make it to better days on the other side.

> ### Tip from Shaf – Where's There's Trouble, There Are Opportunities
>
> From an entrepreneur's point of view, other companies being 100% cash conscious, and worried sick about it, can provide fantastic opportunities. Of course you have to have access to the cash, either in a bank account or as a previously arranged facility.

Even in the hard times, however, the best salesmen will tell you from experience that it's better to walk away from a sale rather than make too great a concession. 'Too great' depends on what's at stake of course. Massive discounts on products or businesses may seem like a better option than going bust but there is a fine line where you discount something so much it will never be seen as having value again.

Another common problem is that people get so involved in a negotiation that they end up thinking they must make this deal at all costs. Be clear in your mind that there will always be another deal, another business to buy or another seller further down the line. If you are not really convinced of that then you are entirely at the mercy of the other party, and that's not the way to deal.

I tried it and ...

I'm an inveterate investor and have always bought properties, thinking that I've made some pretty good deals, which I have. But, looking back on them, I realize that I was always so keen to make the deal that I never really kept to the 'walk away' rule. Truth be told, I had always known from the moment I started negotiating that I was pretty sure to end up making the deal and would be happy if I wrung the slightest price concession out of the sellers. I've since made it a rule to stop looking at property as if I was going to make it my home and only start to look at things where the price is interesting. But I am ready to move on to the next deal if they aren't ready to give me 10% off that asking price straight away. Of course the answer is often 'no' but the ones that have said 'yes' have completely changed my bottom line.

Tip from Shaf – Know When to Stop

Don't let negotiations carry on too long. If you follow all the advice in this chapter then you will always have a very clear idea of your last price and the things you won't budge on, so if those figures are what you're up against there's nothing to be gained from letting the person in front of you keep chipping away at them. You may end up abandoning your own 'non-negotiables' just because you let the other person wear you down with protracted discussions. So set a point to make a final offer. This should be a real final offer, not a gambit or a piece of showmanship. It should represent the very most you're prepared to concede. The final offer is the last play, remember; it's part of the sacred rule that you must always be able to walk away. If that final offer doesn't work then you will only lose by carrying on the negotiation, so it's time to walk away. Of course you can always walk away leaving that offer on the table for the other party to think about but, whatever you do, don't stay there and keep hammering on over the same points you've failed to agree on so far.

Do you know the tricks of the trade?

You will know by now that I do not regard smart negotiating tactics as a substitute for good preparation. There are no tricks that outweigh the worth of getting the basics right. I still think that anyone who has a clear idea of what they want, who has done their homework, and who is ready to walk away if they don't get what they want is the person that's going to do best in nine out of ten negotiations. But if the basics are 90% of negotiating, that still leaves 10% of what you might call the 'craft' of negotiating.

Never be the first to name a price

If you're buying something you should have a price in mind already. In other words, you've already done your homework in order to work out the value of the business in question. You know what you can afford and what you'd really like to pay. But don't just blurt out a figure because the person opposite you asks 'how much?' I always like to let the other party set the ball rolling because that way I can't lose. If they come out with a figure that's too high I have the upper hand because I've done my homework

FAQ – Putting up the Price

Q: *I'm running my own business and my customers are big companies. I keep getting beaten down on pricing thanks to the credit crunch. I'm now getting the impression things are getting better and want to go back to a number of important customers and negotiate a higher price for any future deals. I'm nervous about losing the business – what should I do?*

A: This is a common problem, but really it goes back to the basics. Go over your figures again to be clear how much money you need, and how much you would really like. Then do your market research and find out how that compares to other companies in the same line of business. If you find that you're asking more than them then be clear of what extra value you are adding. If you're confident that your figures add up and what you want to ask is reasonable and competitive given the unique business advantage you bring then you should go back and ask for your new price. If you're still hesitant at this point then ask youself if you're letting personality get in the way of professionalism. Are you perhaps naturally hesitant about asking for more? If you are it might make you a nice person to know, but leave the shame at home when it comes to negotiations. It's not about you, it's about the deal and if you've done your homework and the deal is good you have a duty not to sell it short.

and I can always turn on my heel and walk. If, however, as often happens, they don't really know the worth of what they've got and they come out with a figure that's lower than the starting point you had in mind, you've saved yourself money right from the off.

If you cannot avoid being first to name a price, however, go high when you are selling and low when you are buying, so that the other party has to adjust their thinking because the first number tabled is outside the range that they had prepared for.

Don't fall for the confidence trick

There are plenty of people out there who do well in negotiations because they have the knack of giving off a sense of unlimited confidence. They just so obviously already know how things are going to go, and that means things are going to go their way. For example, they might ask for far more than you were expecting, or they smile and tell you that there's something crucial about this deal that obviously you haven't fully grasped. They're hoping to dent your confidence and put you on the back foot so you doubt yourself and start to wonder if they're right and you should revise your offer. Well don't.

There are plenty of people out there who do well in negotiations because they have the knack of giving off a sense of unlimited confidence.

If you've done your homework as suggested earlier, it's much harder for anyone to pull the confidence trick on you. If they say there's something you haven't understood then get them to explain it to you so you can weigh up that factor, but if you have an armoury of facts and figures at your fingertips you'll find you can usually blow their arguments out of the water. Rolling over people by using the confidence trick is the oldest tactic in the book and it often masks the fact that behind the smile there is a big hole where the solid argument and basic numbers should be. This is why those with the weakest business argument are so often the ones that come up with a price you can barely believe. Don't underestimate the cheek of others when it comes to setting prices.

Tip from Shaf – Telephone Tactics

I do a lot of negotiating on the telephone. I talk to suppliers, customers, people trying to sell me businesses and properties, my managers and so on. If you're not an experienced telephone negotiator you would probably be wise to obey a simple rule – don't make concessions in the same phone call as the other person introduces them.

A good telephone technique is to tie minor issues together. If you're not prepared for someone to suddenly tie, for example, who is going to pay for the low loader to deliver the crane with who is responsible for the insurance of the crane until it's delivered, you can find you've made a concession that you would not have done if you'd had a bit more thinking time. Until you've built your telephone negotiating experience up when asked for a new concession or the other person is tying two or three together, firmly but politely say that you will call back later with an answer. If they insist on an answer there and then they could be trying to hassle you into making a mistake in order to get the deal done in that call.

Practice the look

Some negotiators prefer to call this 'the flinch'. It's that moment when someone puts an offer on the table and you want to make it clear that you're expecting them to budge on the price, or the terms. First impressions really count here and you start sending out signals long before you open your mouth. Some negotiators wince or flinch at the first offer to show that they just aren't going to go for it. You could say it's the 'confidence' trick turned around and they are radiating the fact that this offer is just badly thought out or not worth the money.

I prefer to give it a moment's silence while the offer sinks in. Thanks to the Den, people think I always reply to an offer with a series of questions delivered in a machine gun style. The reason I respond like this sometimes is actually because I'm not really interested and I'm trying to show why by pointing out the real worth of what's on the table. If I am interested I'm often a lot quieter, partly because I'm digesting what I'm being told, and partly because of the principle of the pregnant pause.

Negotiation is a tense moment for most of us and people get more nervous when it all goes quiet. If someone is pitching to me and I fall silent then it usually makes them think that they've overdone it and set the price too high or not offered me a big enough stake. If, in their heart of hearts, they already know they're asking too much, then the silence will usually be the first step to make them back away from that initial demand.

Leave your sense of shame at home

I was once told that if you don't feel slightly embarrassed by the initial offer you make then you're offering too much. The point is that because we tend to put ourselves in the shoes of others we want to make the kind of offer we'd like to receive. Now negotiating doesn't have to be about one person winning and one person losing – the idea is that you both get what you want, but if you're always making the kind of offer you'd like to receive then you will end up paying too much. Remember that we're not talking about buying carpets in a bazaar here. Pay too much for an object and you can quietly forget about it but pay too much for a business and you've just damaged all your future figures for profit and loss. A carpet remains a carpet whatever you pay but pay too much for a business and it can stop being a realistic concern right there. So be prepared to be a bit hard-nosed when it comes to price and don't be ashamed about haggling for a lower price if it boosts your margins and leaves you more money for operating costs. This brings me to the next point.

Separate the personal from the professional

My way of doing business relies a lot on gut feeling and, as I said in Chapter 4, I invest in people not products. That doesn't mean, however, that I let personality get in the way of the deal. I might like the person, but if I don't like the deal they're proposing then I make it clear that I would only like to work with them if they can come up with another deal for me. It works the other way too. Passing over a good deal because you don't especially get on with the other party is not good business sense. Getting heated about a business deal is usually a sign that you're taking it personally and that's not good business sense either.

By its very nature, being an entrepreneur depends a lot on being a good negotiator. Mind you, everyone in business is a negotiator, but the difference is that entrepreneurs are continuously both buying and selling, so they're the head of both the sales division and the purchasing division.

Time now to go into selling mode and consider getting to the exit – selling a business.

SELL BUSINESSES FOR A PROFIT

I f you were selling a house you wouldn't show it to prospective buyers while the plumbing was leaking, the paint was peeling off the walls, and the kid's toys were scattered across the floor. Well not if you wanted to get the best price for it, that's for sure. Selling a business isn't so very different. Don't put in all the work of building a business and then get a poor price for it because you can't get round to fixing, for example, those dodgy staff appraisals before the buyers investigate.

Most of us have heard about the tricks of selling a house. We basically know that you never recover your money on fixtures and fittings, or home improvements, but at the same time there are some things that you can do. You can add to the selling price and secure a faster sale by investing in a lick of paint, or tearing out that dated old carpet and laying a cheap but clean-looking wooden laminate floor. We automatically realize that having broken windows, or an old car on bricks in the driveway, is the kiss of death for the sale.

Yet, when it comes to businesses, there are so many people trying to sell them with the equivalent of rusting hulks out the front and nasty chills blowing through unplugged holes. In this chapter I'm going to point out to you what you need to fix, and what you need to clear out altogether, in order to have a sellable business. Finally, I'm going to give you a few pointers of fine polishing to help smooth your sale – the equivalent of filling a house you want to sell with the smells of freshly baked bread and newly brewed coffee.

Do you know why you're selling?

There isn't a business owner alive who hasn't dreamt of selling their business. Just as millions of office-bound workers dream of quitting their jobs and going it alone, so business owners dream of the day when unreliable suppliers, bad payers, seasonal dips, and the minefields of modern marketing are no longer problems to haunt them in the early hours. Even highly successful entrepreneurs, particularly in the UK, dream of getting out and going back to the simple life – usually one where leisure, sun-kissed beaches and happy family lives all play a significant part. So much so in fact that it's a well-established fact of the UK entrepreneur market that a lot of serious entrepreneurs are actually back in business having made enough money to retire and done the round-the-world cruise.

They've already set up successful businesses, and sold out for at least the magic million mark. (It's funny how we still dream of being 'millionaires' even though a million barely buys you a house with a garden in a decent part of Edinburgh these days. If being a millionaire was your aspiration five years ago, you better up the ante.)

Anyway these people have made it, life is good, and they can relax now. Except they can't; or at least the good ones can't. In the UK you get a lot of folk who 'make it' then realize that it was never just about having the money to pay off the mortgage and buy a yacht. They really miss the thrill of running a business.

Most of all they miss the strategic thinking and buzz of playing the game, trading one business for another in the search of further success. But at the end of the day if all you really want to do is sell up and go fishing then that's fine, we're all different.

If you're selling up to get out of the game or as part of a plan to cash in your chips and move to a bigger game, then a lot of the ground rules are still the same. However, you must be absolutely clear in your head which type of these two sellers you are. Don't think it's going to be easy either, because people bidding for your business will demand no end of information and you'll need an answer for every question.

The obvious question to start with is 'why do you want to sell it?' If it's because you fancy retiring and growing prize marrows then great, because that's the kind of answer many people might want to hear. But don't expect anyone to believe that if you're in your twenties (or for that matter if you're a Scottish multimillionaire known for speculating).

... people bidding for your business will demand no end of information and you'll need an answer for every question.

So given that you're not retiring, what is your reason for selling? You might be thinking that you've reached a dead end and that the business is either going to stay still or start to decline. In this case then it's likely to be sniffed out by potential buyers who will either lower their bid or walk away. You really need to get the business into a condition where you can, hand on heart, tell people that while you are confident about the business and its future, you desperately want to focus on another project that's got you more excited in a different direction, for example. This had better be the truth and you'd better be able to give evidence of the secure future of the business you are selling because the buyer won't stop probing until they've found out what's really going on.

A lot of people put their business on the market, and then take it off again after a while because they haven't got the offers they were hoping for. Try not to do this. Be clear in your mind about why it's the right time now to sell this particular business and what you want to do with the money you raise.

Of course if it really is a terrible time to sell the business then you may have to hang on in there for a while. To be honest I think that anyone who only finds that their timing is bad when they put their business on the market just hasn't done their home-work. Another reason for sales falling through is that sellers haven't spent enough time thinking about the sale from the point of view of the buyer. Stop thinking about that yacht/car/next investment for a minute and instead put yourself in the shoes of someone coming round to look at the business with a view to buying.

Ask yourself:

- what's in it for them?
- why should they buy?
- is it fairly valued (see Chapter 6)?
- is it going anywhere?
- could it easily increase its value if it were bought by someone with more money for investment, with synergy in suppliers or customers or with better logistics or routes to market?

If you've already considered the turnaround strategies of Chapter 7 then you should be in a good position to explain to someone else:

- what needs to be done to build the profitability of the business
- why you're not the right person to do that right now
- why they are.

If you've got that thinking straight then you're already much closer to making the sale.

Whatever you do, don't take a sale too lightly. It's not like a house. There are plenty of people who put their house on the market to see what it might bring in and take it off again after finding how much it's worth. That just causes mild irritation for estate agents and potential buyers.

Try this, however, with a business and you have to be aware that just putting it up for sale will have an immediate effect on staff morale, suppliers, customers (don't think word won't get out), bankers and your future business partners. You can take it back off the market if you think you're not getting the offers you want, but you'll never get it out of the minds of all the people involved that you're looking to get out. Like an employee who tries to re-sign and is talked out of it you'll never be seen as having the same level of commitment. This could end up having a negative effect on the value of the very thing you're trying to flog.

So seriously:

- know why you're selling
- know why you're selling now
- know who will get benefits out of the business if they buy it now
- know the answers to all the questions they are going to ask.

If you don't know the above, then for goodness sake find out fast or forget about the sale.

Are you clear about what it is you're selling?

You're selling the business right? Well, yes, but what is the business? You might have one idea of what it is that's for sale here, but your potential buyer might have another. This can cause problems. You don't want to waste valuable business selling time clarifying all of that because:

- it takes time and effort
- at the end of the discussion you may find you're not talking about the same thing.

So let's get a few things straight right from the start. There are a number of ways of selling a company. You can sell the whole thing, lock stock and smoking liabilities. You can just sell the assets. Or you can sell shares in the company. Or, if you've left it all too late (you shouldn't have, if you've followed the rest of the book), then you may be looking to liquidate the whole thing as painlessly as possible. Take a moment and consider the options.

Look, finding a buyer is difficult and needs some preparation. Small, privately held businesses are unlikely to interest financial buyers like private equity and venture capital firms. So the two most likely exits would be trade sales and management buy-out.

Trade sales

This is probably the first thing you think of when it comes to selling up, and with good reason as it often offers by far the easiest sale and best return. In a trade sale you sell the business to someone else who intends to run it pretty much as it is. One pub owner sells to another pub owner, that sort of thing.

In this case, look for the reverse of what you were doing when you were buying businesses, searching for synergies where, for example, common customers or suppliers made the sum of two businesses greater than the value of the two separately. This, of course, has an impact on the price of the deal. If you can recognize the benefits of the merger to the buyer due to synergies, so

Tip from Shaf – Who Should I Sell To?

Don't just put the business up for sale and see who bites; you'll get a better price if you think about who would want it and then go directly to those people. Things to think about include the possibility that:

- your customers could be worth more than your business – a new entrant to a market may be prepared to pay over the odds for access to customers just to leapfrog their way into serious contention

- one of your products may be the piece that fits the gap in someone else's product range

- you have the distribution solution to their manufacturing needs

- economies of scale could mean the difference between long-term survival and failure for a company that is relatively cash rich but struggling with its profit margins

- don't forget to look abroad for your potential buyer – your business might be the perfect stepping stone into the UK market for a continental competitor.

that two and two make five, then you can base the price you want on the profits of the new combined concern rather than the old one.

To do all this requires some preparation work.

- Do everything possible to let other firms in your field know that you exist. Join trade bodies and raise your company profile in the year or so leading up to the planned exit time.

(Mind you, if you take my advice you will have done this long before you're ready to sell.) Study the market and draw up a short list of buyers to whom an acquisition may make sense. Particularly look for people who have already made acquisitions – it's habit forming. Make sure they know your company and what it does. Study their structure and re-engineer your own company so that there are obvious synergies and as painless a merger as you can plan.

- Nurture a relationship with the trade press and set some resource aside to get PR in the lead up to exit. Trade magazines are always hungry for stories, however mundane; they have white space to fill every day or every week. Make sure you feed them. Speak to local network contacts in banks, local accountants and so on. But, beware of giving the business a bad name by touting it around too heavily or for too long.

- Get a company name check. You could hit problems if you share a name with another company, no matter how small or obscure.

- Raise your profile. To get the high profile so useful in making a sale, join the Institute of Directors, or perhaps the local Round Table.

- Look in trade journals for companies looking to buy businesses. You can advertise for a buyer yourself, of course, but you'll find it is mostly bars, bed and breakfast places and newsagents who use this route.

- Make it obvious that your business will fit under their management structure and that subsequent salary savings justify the price paid. In the last year or two make sure profitability looks good so that you're selling from strength. Work up to what we might call a 'selling' set of accounts. Freeze or reduce your shareholders' salaries and take dividends instead to enhance the bottom line. Keep all unnecessary expenses down to maximize profits as the price agreed is likely to be based on a multiplier of the past year's profits (see below). Remember that bad assets, such as bad debts or duff stock, taint the good assets, so get the balance sheet as clean as you can.

- Make sure that the business won't need you as an individual in the long term. This would make the business a going concern separate from you and therefore of higher value. Remember, for example, that sales that depend on personal relationships are worthless to the buyer, so make sure your customers are sewn in to the company and not to you personally.

- Approach potential buyers from the past. If you have had approaches from potential buyers before, now is the time to follow them up and see if you can rekindle interest.

Remember, for example, that sales that depend on personal relationships are worthless to the buyer, so make sure your customers are sewn in to the company and not to you personally.

Management buy-outs and management buy-ins

A management buy-out is where your own management, keen to continue running the company themselves, offers to buy you out. You convert your stake of the company into shares and sell that to them in return for the money. Done well, this means that you get to walk away to pursue your new interests while those people who care enough and whose jobs are at stake get to keep their jobs and continue working on building the company. You can prepare for this by identifying and recruiting ambitious and dynamic executives who could attract institutional investors. In practice this can be a huge hurdle to overcome. To buy you out, the managers will have to raise money and the people who lend it to them may well insist that you retain a role as an executive director. What this means is that you don't truly get shot of the old company. (Arguably this is better than the alternative where they may insist that you have no further role in the company at all, leaving you with the distinct impression that they're glad to get shot of you.)

Prepare for this route by talking to private equity companies and venture capital firms well ahead of buy-out time. Doing this will enable you to know what they are looking for and perhaps change your strategy to cater for that in the future.

A management buy-in, on the other hand, is where an outside management team buys a stake in your company and replaces the existing management. Since the current staff will lose their jobs and the whole process is an admission that things have not been well handled, you're not likely to get such a good deal. Again private equity firms and venture capitalists may have a management team that they could bring in. This would solve your problem as to who will run the company without you and make the transaction more attractive to investors. But all of this comes at a price – the more you need other people to make this happen for you, the less you will get in your share of the deal.

As in all things to do with business, fashion plays a major role. At one time there can be a passion for spreading company risk by diversifying into new business areas and building a conglomerate. At other times the mantra may well be 'break the monoliths up.' Make sure you know what is hot right now. In simple terms this means that the company you are looking for will either be looking to get into another business sector or looking to expand their current activities. The key is to understand what is fashionable right now and develop your selling strategy accordingly. (I have found that selling a company to a conglomerate that is unfamiliar with your business sector may well get you a better price.)

Stock market floatation

What are capital markets? Capital markets exist for the benefit of companies and investors. In their primary role they enable organizations to raise new long-term finance – this helps companies. In their secondary role they help investors by providing a market place for the trading of securities.

Most small listings are issued by placing. The issuer, normally a merchant bank and a stockbroker, place the shares with their clients. Large issues are normally by Offer for sale, or Offer for sale by tender. In the first case the company offers the shares at a price, in the second the shares are sold by auction. In almost all cases the issue is underwritten, which means that financial institutions agree to buy any unsold shares for a fixed fee. This takes the risk out of the share issue as far as the company raising the finance is concerned. It is, of course, very expensive to remove the risk. Their fees are high.

This option of a way out is only really a possibility for those who have built a pretty substantial business, trading for at least three years and of a certain size. However, remember that while 'floatation' usually makes everybody think of the London Stock Exchange there are two other stock markets in the UK which are intended for smaller companies. The Alternative Investment Market (AIM) and in specialist markets PLUS might be worth a look, if you are confident that the effort involved in exchanging part of your stake into investor money is worth the time and money it will cost you to do so. Mind you, there is a lot of free advice available on floating and one of the best sources is at www.londonstockexchange.com, where you can get information on when is the right time to float all the way to what you have to do to join the main market or AIM.

Floating on the stock market sounds deeply exciting and in the right climate it can be. The right climate is usually one in which shares are trading freely and fast and optimism is high. Take a good look around you and tell me if you think that's the case right now ...

Besides the questionable wisdom of floating a company at a time like this, you should be aware that compared to a trade sale it involves a great deal more due diligence, paperwork, accountants and lawyers, none of whom work for free.

On the plus side it's a great motivator for staff; they will be able to buy or be given shares and think about become a part owner of the company's profits as well as a contributor to them. On the negative side you'll find that it means selling control of your company and you'll find your boardroom populated with strange faces telling you what to do. A number of notable companies have tried being public companies and then gone back to private ownership by borrowing the money to buy it back. They normally give their reasons as being that they were unable to deal with the other shareholders looking over their shoulders. Perhaps the highest profile example of this is Richard Branson, who did exactly that.

Use venture capitalists as a stepping-stone to floatation

Venture capitalists have a fund of money that they put into a series of high-risk enterprises. They look for a new venture that is too risky for traditional bank lending and their finance is often known as 'ground floor' or 'early stage' investment. Since it is high risk it is also expensive, and the owners of the business will have to offer equity in the business to the venture people who will also probably want to put a director on the board.

The venture capitalist will look for an 'exit route' within, say, three years. Remember they only expect 10% of their ventures to blossom. This tends to put them predominantly into the high technology area where the eventual returns can be huge. Huge is a good word to use in relation to venture capitalists – they want to invest big money in adventurous enterprises.

The venture capitalist will try to structure a deal so that the management has a strong incentive to work hard. They may have to put up with modest salaries, lower perhaps than they could get working for someone else. They will also talk of 'equity ratchets' whereby there is a transfer of equity from the venture capitalist to the entrepreneurs if performance targets are met, or vice versa if they are not.

And if you do get venture capital money make sure you don't get the business into difficulties. If you do the venture capitalists will put all sorts of advisers in to protect their position. These advisers take up a lot of time asking management questions, producing reports and charging high fees for the privilege.

Sell some shares in your company to an interested company
Before you start selling off the whole company, or the assets of it, consider the possibility of selling a share of the company – you can do this by selling some of your existing shares in the company or creating new ones. You need an accountant here to advise. *Dragons' Den Online* is all about people coming to us and trying to sell a stake in their business in return for a wad of investment cash. Or at least that's the theory. The reality is that there's a lot more at stake than the £50,000 that sits on the table next to me each time. The real value comes from the mentoring that the successful candidates get along with the money. They're not just selling a stake in the company; they're exchanging it for

the business savvy that got me and fellow Dragon Julie into that Den in the first place.

They're not just selling a stake in the company; they're exchanging it for the business savvy that got me and fellow Dragon Julie into that Den in the first place.

Selling a stake in the company to a business 'angel' who not only stumps up cash but can take you to the next level is often a very good way to go. Be careful about what it is you're selling here, because it comes back to the question of whether you're an entrepreneur, an inventor, or a manager. A really good angel/ Dragon will almost certainly expect the dragon's share of your business. They will take control of the business in return for offering you that breakthrough you're looking for. This means that you'd better be clear about whether that next step is worth it. If it's the step you need to improve earnings and gain the recognition required for your next venture then why would you not sell the majority of your company? You're only going to be moving on to other things in any case anyway ...

Or are you worried that you've sold your soul? In this case, you might want to think about one particular aspect of selling your company: selling yourself.

Paint yourself out of the picture

Unless you want to be running the same company for the rest of your life you should take steps to ensure that you are no longer essential to it. In a lot of cases the entrepreneur sells their company only to find that there's a lock-in clause of anywhere from six months to several years in which they are expected to continue working at the company. If it's just six months then the purpose of this is probably to ease the transition, which is fine; but if it stretches out to years then you've sold yourself in the process of selling your business. Quite simply the buyer believes that the company doesn't have the same value without you (and/or other key staff) and so they will not do the deal unless those people are thrown in. Usually this lock-in is made sweeter with all the usual bribes of salary, bonuses, shares, etc. but I would say that for the true entrepreneur it is a gilded cage. If you've got what it takes to keep on moving to the next level of the game then you don't want to be tied down just as you're starting out with the investment money made from your first sale. But also bear in mind that the business itself is probably worth more if the buyer doesn't need to buy you along with it. So find a way to make yourself disposable if you really want to sell up and move on.

Tip from Shaf – Making Yourself Disposable

There are three main things that can make you look so important to a company that a potential buyer will think that the company without you will not be a going concern with growth possibilities.

- Your relationships with your customers – make sure you have passed these on by introducing the person who is taking over and referring the customer to them every time they contact you.

- Your relationships with suppliers – the same goes here. The key is to make the supplier feel that they are doing business with the company not with you.

- Your relationship with your people – this will only break a possible deal if there is a faint suspicion that some key people will leave to go with you. Be open about this. If you are hoping to take some people with you, then make that clear and show the potential buyer how their contribution will be replaced.

Have you prepared the business for sale?

Once you've sorted out what you're selling, why you're selling it and how you're selling it, it's time to answer all those questions that a buyer might ask, as well as doing the housework to get the place spick and span, and finally discretely painting yourself out of the picture both to ease the sale and leave you free when the deed is done.

Valuing the business

Chapter 6 should have given you a good idea of just how much your business is worth, but be aware that there are many different ways of valuing a business and you might want to think about a few of them so that you can counter any different valuations when negotiating with buyers.

Earnings multiplier

The most likely way anyone is going to put a price on your work is a multiple of future earnings. However, before you get carried away and start multiplying up the biggest figure you can think of, remember that most buyers will be looking for 'sustainable' profits which means that first you must 'normalize' earnings by adjusting any unusual sales or profit periods to give a more realistic picture. If you're lucky enough to be selling a well-established and successful company you may find buyers who prefer to skip earnings and instead focus on cash flow multipliers. Again be aware that this isn't simply a matter of multiplying to find that big fat figure you have in mind – most calculations reduce future estimates of cash flow on what you might call the 'bird in hand' basis; cash flow now is worth more than predicted cash flow some time in the future.

Asset valuation

If the business isn't going too well but it happens to be in an elegant Victorian warehouse facing onto a canal near a city centre then you might want to forget about cash flow and profits altogether and instead focus on an asset valuation. Generally, of course, the value of a company is related directly to its profits last year and its expectations of profits in the future. But sometimes the valuation is as much about the value of the assets as its potential profitability. Remember again that it's not all good news, so 'bad' assets will be taken into account against good – but we'll come to the detail of that later.

Like for like

This isn't so much a formal way of evaluating a business as an arguing tactic when you're in negotiations but if you're selling into the trade – especially someone in a very similar line of business – then do some figures on what it would cost to build a similar business from scratch. Once you've worked out what it would cost to hire the staff, buy the equipment, find the premises, acquire the customers etc., you have a pretty good figure to throw into negotiations when things get stuck.

Once you've worked out what it would cost to hire the staff, buy the equipment, find the premises, acquire the customers etc., you have a pretty good figure to throw into negotiations when things get stuck.

Gut feeling and guesses

Despite all the different formula in the world, it is also the case that, like anything else in this world, your company is worth what a buyer is ready to pay for it. Which means that valuing a business isn't just about totting up the figures and multiplying the projections (though you'd better not forget to do that too), it's also about thinking carefully about why someone else would want to pay for it and what sort of factors will affect them.

That means taking into account such things as the general economic climate and how bullish (or bearish) your market sector is right now. This is likely to include how well your company controls costs and in particular how it manages cash flow. It certainly includes the price paid for any other similar businesses recently (rather like the housing market), so do your homework and if you think your business is worth more than recent sales, have your arguments prepared. It is also affected by any number of intangible factors such as customer and supplier goodwill, the presence/absence and lifespan of patents you may have on any products.

One of the first questions I ask any inventor in the Den is if they have a patent and I never take the answer 'yes' unless they show me the patent itself. Getting a patent is quite a laborious process and people can claim they have done it when they are actually just on the foothills. Buyers will also look at how well the current management has steered the business around difficulties in the past, so you'll need to discuss whether they're buying the staff as well. Most of all, you'll need to be clear about whether they're buying how much of you.

Get an expert

Finally you may want to get an expert in to provide an unbiased valuation. That's a bit like getting a surveyor's report on a house and has a number of benefits:

- you get the benefit of seeing your business through someone else's eyes
- you get a heads up on things that may need changing before you approach a buyer

- you get to talk/argue price with someone else before there's real money on the table
- you have a better legal standing if there any post-sale shenanigans or arguments.

FAQ – Agents

Q: *My business is extremely well known locally and in my market, so I'm loathe to put feelers out in my area about selling it in case it's recognized. I've heard there are agents out there who can do the job for me and make approaches around the country (and even outside it) and that because they represent so many other companies the whole thing is much more likely to be discrete. What do you think?*

A: Agents can be a blessing or a curse. On the one hand it's great to have someone else doing the legwork for you but on the other hand it means you're a step away from the whole process. I prefer to be involved in my own business and I personally don't find that agents know as much about my business as I do. They can save you time, and if you really have to be discrete they can help ensure your anonymity, but when it comes to evaluating your company be prepared for some surprises and a few arguments to boot.

Put the books in order

Don't be one of those candidates in the Den that stutters and implodes when I ask the hard questions about money. If you think you might be, review Chapter 6 again until you can talk the language. Buyers want clear answers and one of the easiest ways to blow a deal is to seem vague or unclear about your finances. Audit your books, talk through them with your accountant and ask him/her what leaps off the page as a problem so you can talk it through to prepare for the same discussion in front of a potential buyer. That means that everything, including balance sheets, assets, liabilities, money you're owed, borrowings and tax position (including any likely future charges) should all be on paper, clean and clear, and open for scrutiny. Do anything less and you're just asking for the sale to fall through.

Now think about what isn't there in black and white on the profit and loss account. Do you have sales/distribution agreements that exist between you and a long-established partner? Are they contractually binding? A relationship that has worked since the dawn of time is no good to a potential buyer if it is based on goodwill that may go out of the door when you do. So make sure everything that is essential to the business is contractually binding and signed and sealed.

Other points to remember are thorny issues like compliance with regulations. That doesn't just mean keeping clear of money laundering and gun running but increasingly it means the likes of 'green' regulations on power consumption, and recycling of old goods. Perhaps you haven't quite had the time to get up to speed on compliance – you've had a business to run after all – but you can be sure that your buyer will be aware of the issues, and will probably have a figure in mind of how much it will cost to set the issue to rights. To top it all you don't want to be sitting there with your mouth open when a buyer tells you that Brussels is imposing a future standard on your industry which will cost you a pretty penny to comply with – a figure which is naturally going to be subtracted from your price. I've said it before, but I'll say it again – do your homework.

Again, you may want to consider getting an independent third party in to check the books and see if everything is in order. This shows that you're up front and it often throws up problems that you'd be better off smoothing out before sitting down with a buyer.

Beware also the administration that goes with having staff. Consult a Human Resources person and see what is necessary legally. It may be that at the size you are now you need a formal appraisal system, job descriptions and so on. These things always seem a big burden if you haven't done them before; but if you turn your mind to them you'll probably find it comes quite easily. It should not be expensive to buy the formal stuff in and get a bit of advice.

Bin the bad

I mentioned earlier that bad assets will be counted against the good. When a potential business seller walks through a warehouse, they only see the rows of gleaming new stock that are virtually walking out the warehouse doors themselves. A potential buyer on the other hand can only see the piles of rusty old stock that have stood there for a decade and seem to be leaking something green, slimy, and able to burn through steel.

Don't be a hoarder. The time of selling a business means spring-cleaning, and that means being absolutely ruthless with stock. There is always a way of offloading stock somewhere, especially now that the web gives us access to markets we never dreamed of. Best of all you can sell off your unwanted stock without advertising the fact that it's you. Don't forget that even a simple thing like eBay can be used to shift stock. If you find yourself with a large amount of related items you could set up an online shop specifically to sell them or use one of the third party companies that does that for you. Now is not the time to rue the day you bought 14,000 left-handed hammers. Instead, it's the time to think about what that old stock will do to the price of the good stock that sits next to it in the warehouse. Cut your losses and get rid of everything that might look bad to a potential buyer.

One of the companies I have an investment in ran a promotion called 'Buy a Bag o' Crap'. They shifted over 10,000 Bag o' Crap products for £4.99 each, making almost £50,000. Customers are warned that the mystery boxes are full of 'leftover crap' from the company's warehouse – and could be anything from a new TV to empty DVD cases. But the bags became an Internet hit, with customers posting clips of themselves opening their 'gifts' on YouTube. If you can sell a Bag o' Crap you can sell anything.

It's not just industrial waste that can be toxic, debts can be too. Bad debt will leap off the page at a buyer and put them right off. So the best thing is to call in all old debts, however hard that may be, before approaching a seller. Of course the chances are that those debts are proving very hard to call in, that's why they're still on the books after all this time – which means you have some hard decisions to make. If you really can't bring yourself to re-possess Granny Smith's house then think about getting someone else to do it. Or if you're still not comfortable with that (you big softy) then it may be time to *... that was the hard fact and potential buyers will in 99% of cases find that out.* wipe away the debt and write it off rather than risk it interfering with an otherwise profitable sale.

One woman who was looking to sell her business complained when I suggested she wrote off some debts that looked very iffy. 'But,' she said, 'If I do that the business will not look a good enough prospect to buy.' The hard fact was that her business simply was not ready for sale since writing off that debt made the balance sheet look very weak. But that was the hard fact and potential buyers will in 99% of cases find that out.

Put your people in order

Books and fixed assets aren't the only things that need a bit of tidying up before you're ready to sell. People and systems are a big part of the picture too.

You must avoid a situation where your management first find out the news of you selling the company when a potential buyer asks them what they do. That's poor people management. In that situation you're trying to sell a company composed of people who may feel that the rug is about to be pulled out from under their feet.

So tell people what's going on. This might feel a bit like splitting from a lover – with all that 'it's not you it's me' stuff. However, if you know you are selling a going concern in order to move on, then it should be an opportunity for everyone involved to see how they can improve their own lot. Apart from anything else, if you don't tell people that the business is coming on the market then you're not likely to get an offer of a management buy-out, and a buy-out could be the best solution for all concerned. If it's all too emotional then consider whether you really want to sell it all, or if you want to stay on in some way as a shareholder or advisor. One word to the wise on that; if it really is that emotional then staying on as an advisor to a company you once ran can sometimes be a lot more messy and frustrating for you than a clean break.

Take a look at the people in your company, just as you did with the books and the assets, and ask yourself if anyone is indispensable. It may seem harsh but that is what a buyer is going to do anyway. Buyers don't like being dependent on individuals, including yourself, and would rather know there are systems in place for knowledge management and retention that mean the whole thing can keep on running even if key staff leave. In particular they will be looking hard at sales staff. They tend to be a little nomadic and often move on when there are major changes in a company. Make sure that if a salesperson leaves they don't just walk off with all their contacts, and having done that make sure you can show a potential buyer where all the contact information is stored so they can see it for themselves.

How do you 'Do the Deal'?

Once you have your business in order, the next step is to draw up a sales memorandum, the marketing document for your business – it's a sort of glorified brochure. The sales memorandum spells out all the basics: what your business is, where you see it going, how long you've been trading, opportunities in the market and all those key figures for assets, cash flow, etc., that you've carefully prepared. This is the place to point out any key sales points like patents, market leadership, growth potential, etc. Don't be tempted to stretch the truth here but don't be shy either – this is your sales pitch put down on paper. Done that? Good, now all we have to do is find a buyer.

Choosing a buyer

You don't want to wander around your industry like a town crier shouting at the top of your voice that you want to sell your company. There's nothing quite like the perception of an owner selling up and running to drive down the price of a business.

So instead I always prefer to look for trade buyers. Trade journals, as mentioned earlier, carry general adverts that don't specify the details of who and where so you can end up sharing the details with just a select few who have a vested interest in keeping it to themselves. Business advisers and even banks are often a great source of contacts, as are your own customers and suppliers. Don't forget the 'businesses for sale' sites either, particularly for common like-for-like trades such as pubs, B&Bs or newsagents that are likely to be taken over and run in much the same way by chains of companies in the same industry.

If you have an adviser to help, then hand the job over to him or her completely. Not only because it is more discrete, but because you wouldn't believe the amount of time that can be tied up in meeting potential buyers to whittle it down to the serious parties. Keep your own name and the company name out of the picture for as long as you decently can and before you give the game away to someone who seems serious get them to sign a non-disclosure agreement. If they know what they're doing, they will be happy to do this because it's in their own interests to keep things quiet in case their own competition gets wind of what's going on.

I tried it and ...

" I'd thought of selling the company before, but got cold feet and pulled out – fortunately without telling the world what I was up to. I guess I was worried that I was not properly prepared.

After some planning time, I prepared fully and then started to quietly make advances to potential buyers through a trusted business adviser who only identified the company by its turnover and general profitability. We'd really gone through the books with a fine tooth comb so any queries were quickly dealt with and the resulting quality of response was much higher. Those who showed interest felt they were dealing with someone serious and agreed to non-disclosure agreements and, yes, I have now sold the company (and am busy working on the next one).

Like so many other things in business it's the homework that counts. "

You should be in business to make profits and have fun. You can do that by staying in a large company and climbing up the ladder by getting promoted. You can do it also by getting out and doing it yourself – starting up a business and growing it into a thriving concern. But the best profits and fun you can have, at least in my experience, is buying into businesses as well as starting them up, mentoring people to become skilled business people, and then moving on by selling that business and buying others. Building a portfolio of businesses with good people managing them and backing the businesses up with a portfolio of properties is the most fun I've had. So stop looking at the pool from the high board and take the plunge – come on in, the water's terrifying.

APPENDIX

Income From Current Debtors @ 6 Dec	Total	Dec	Jan	Feb	Mar
Customer 1	£30,000	£30,000			
Customer 2	£3,300	£3,300			
Customer 3	£11,500	£6,000	£5,500		
Customer 4	£14,000	£7,000	£7,000		
Customer 5	£5,500	£1,500	£4,000		
Insurance Claim	£3,000			£3,000	
Others	£2,000	£1,000	£1,000		
Debtor Income	**£69,300**	**£48,800**	**£17,500**	**£3,000**	
Expected Sales	Value	Dec	Jan	Feb	Mar
Customer 6	£132,000		£13,000	£44,000	£30,000
Others	£31,000	£31,000			
Total Sales	**£163,000**	**£31,000**	**£13,000**	**£44,000**	**£30,000**
Sales Receipts	Debtors	£48,800	£17,500	£3,000	
From Sales	30 days		£15,500	£6,500	£22,000
From Sales	60 days			£15,500	£6,500
Total Receipts	**£232,300**	**£48,800**	**£33,000**	**£25,000**	**£28,500**
Fixed costs		£11,000	£11,000	£11,000	£11,000
Cost of sales					
Customer 6 @ 20% mark up					
Other @ 20% mark up				£20,000	£25,833
Total Outgoing		**£11,000**	**£31,000**	**£36,833**	**£21,833**
Cashflow Balance		Dec	Jan	Feb	Mar
Bank		£0			
Add sales receipts		£48,800	£33,000	£25,000	£28,500
Reduce by outgoing costs			£11,000	£31,000	£36,833
Cash Position		**£37,800**	**£2,000**	**-£11,833**	**£6,667**
Cumulative		£37,800	£39,800	£27,967	£34,633

Notes

1   The doubtful payer is not shown
2   Uninvoiced retentions of £25,000 not shown, part of which will be incoming over the period shown
3   Receipts from current debtors are agreed payment dates
4   Sales receipts assumed to take : 50% 60 days, 50% 30 days
5   Staff numbers assumed to remain the same
6   Creditors are assumed to be stretched up to 60 days

April	May	June	July	Notes
				1
				2
				3
				4
April	May	June	July	5
£45,000				
				6
£45,000				
£15,000	£22,500			
£22,000	£15,000	£22,500		
£37,000	**£37,500**	**£22,500**		
£11,000	£11,000	£11,000	£11,000	
£10,833	£36,667	£25,000	£37,500	
£47,667	**£36,000**	**£48,500**	**£11,000**	
April	May	June	July	
£37,000	£37,500	£22,500	£0	
£21,833	£47,667	£36,000	£48,500	£11,000
-£10,667	**£1,500**	**-£26,000**	**-£11,000**	
£23,967	£25,467	-£533	-£11,533	

Balance @ End of July   **-£11,533**

Figures shown do not include the effect of VAT

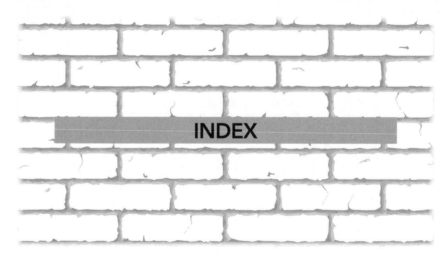

INDEX